PRACTICING CHRISTIAN EDUCATION

AN INTRODUCTION FOR MINISTRY

**Mark A. Maddix
and James Riley Estep Jr.**

Baker Academic
a division of Baker Publishing Group
Grand Rapids, Michigan

© 2017 by Mark A. Maddix and James Riley Estep Jr.

Published by Baker Academic
a division of Baker Publishing Group
PO Box 6287, Grand Rapids, MI 49516-6287
www.bakeracademic.com

Printed in the United States of America

Library of Congress Cataloging-in-Publication Data
Names: Maddix, Mark A., 1965– author.
Title: Practicing Christian education : an introduction for ministry / Mark A. Maddix and James Riley Estep Jr.
Description: Grand Rapids : Baker Academic, 2017. | Includes bibliographical references and index.
Identifiers: LCCN 2016051182 | ISBN 9780801030963 (pbk.)
Subjects: LCSH: Christian education. | Teaching. | Theology—Study and teaching. | Education (Christian theology) | Church work.
Classification: LCC BV1471.3 .M25 2017 | DDC 268—dc23
LC record available at https://lccn.loc.gov/2016051182

Scripture quotations are from The Holy Bible, English Standard Version® (ESV®), copyright © 2001 by Crossway, a publishing ministry of Good News Publishers. Used by permission. All rights reserved. ESV Text Edition: 2011

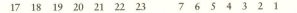
17 18 19 20 21 22 23   7 6 5 4 3 2 1

green
press
INITIATIVE

Contents

Illustrations and Tables

The Value
of Christian Education

C. S. Lewis's *Mere Christianity* speaks to the value of Christian education. In fact, it speaks to the absolute necessity of education in the Christian faith. He speaks of approaching the complexities of modern life with "boys' philosophies" and a "child's religion." Embracing a simple faith works for a while, but when we're faced with the complexities of adult life, the basic, underdeveloped, rudimentary teachings of childhood don't seem to adequately respond to life's reality. Lewis further observes, "Very often, however, this silly procedure is adopted by people who are not silly, but who, consciously or unconsciously, want to destroy Christianity. Such people put up a version of Christianity suitable for a child of six and make that the object of their attack." In other words, Christian doctrine is complex and some are unwilling to study and embrace its complexities.[1] Sound familiar?

Decades later, John G. Stackhouse echoed the same concern in his *Evangelical Landscapes*, wherein he stresses the importance of Christians knowing and living their faith. He observes, "Evangelicals used to be accused of being 'biblicistic' and even 'bibliolatrous' as they reflexively referred any problem of life to a Bible text. That accusation can rarely be leveled anymore, and it is not necessarily because evangelicals have become more theologically sophisticated. Many instead have become just as ignorant of the Bible as anyone else."[2] However, he later comments,

This is the work of theology, and it is work every Christian must do: learning what God has said and learning how to say it for oneself in one's Christian community. The ignorance of the general public about the fundamentals of the Christian faith is regrettable. The ignorance of churchgoing Christians about the fundamentals of the Christian faith, however, is scandalous. Christians are somehow expected to think and feel and live in a distinctive way, as followers of Jesus, without being provided the basic vocabulary, grammar, and concepts of the Christian religion.[3]

How can someone have a genuine walk with Christ—be a *Christian*—if they do not know the faith, value the faith, and know how to practice the faith? *They cannot!* Stackhouse cautions us against trying to be a Christian in the absence of knowing Scripture, while C. S. Lewis calls us to be continuing students of Scripture, not settling for a faith suited only for a child. *Christian education* is the church's response to the need for a growing, vibrant, practical faith. It is like electricity. No one notices it until it doesn't work. We often do not value education until we realize we are ill prepared or unequipped to give a faithful response to life's challenges. We are not talking about Sunday school, small groups, or Bible studies. These are forms or programs of Christian education. So what is Christian education itself, and why is it so vital?

What Is Education?

Education can be described as an activity of teaching, something parents, teachers, pastors, and institutions *do*. Some may focus on the learner, defining education as a *process* or becoming educated. Others define education by the finished *product*; what did you get from school? An education. It can also be defined as a discipline, the content studied. Thus we can say that education is the study of subjects. It may be too simple, but in fact, all these different definitions have one element in common. *Education results in learning.* Wherever learning is occurring, education is occurring. But not all education is the same; it's not all about classes.

The concept of education exists along a spectrum, as depicted in table 1.1. The spectrum goes from formal to nonformal to informal education, and shows the learning associated with each type of education.

What happens when this is confused? Don't let the terms confuse you. For example, Sunday school is not really a "school," or at least it shouldn't be. Schools are institutions of formal learning, with the assumption that if students are in the fourth-grade class, they have already been through the first- through third-grade classes. However, Sunday school cannot make this

Table 1.1 Spectrum of Education

Formal ←————→	Nonformal ←————→	Informal
1. Intentional instruction 2. Overt curriculum 3. Structured organization 4. Institutional 5. Low immediate application 6. Typically long-term	1. Intentional instruction 2. Overt curriculum 3. Semi-structured organization 4. Noninstitutional 5. Immediate application 6. Typically short-term	1. Typically unintentional 2. Hidden curriculum 3. Unstructured 4. Society/culture based 5. Immediate application 6. Lifelong
Schooling; attending a Christian school or university	*Seminar*; receiving training for ministry or participating in a supervised internship	*"School of hard knocks"*; life experience, personal engagement with culture and society
Example: Progressing toward a bachelor's degree and passing the prescribed four-year sequence of courses at a Christian university	*Example*: Taking a four-session training program for teachers at church to develop teaching and improve classroom-management skills	*Example*: Learning when to bow your head, be silent, or stand up in a worship service based on the example of others
Church-based program: Bible institute	*Church-based program*: Adult Bible fellowship, small groups	*Church-based program*: Socialization, opportunities to build relationships

assumption. Sunday school should have more of a nonformal approach, with an emphasis on immediate application. When it comes to learning, these three forms of education serve different purposes, all necessary. Figure 1.1 illustrates this. The larger circle is "learning" in general; it's what we "know." Informal education contributes the most; however, we often don't realize it. We learn much of our morals, dispositions, cultural assumptions, and social conventions from informal learning, picked up as we go through life or become members of the church. Formal education is the second-largest circle, primarily because of the duration of formal learning. Consider that a student in college spends an estimated eighteen hundred hours in the classroom and a projected thirty-six hundred hours in study, preparation, and completing assignments for class, all within a four-year period of time. Formal education also tends to be larger, broader in scope, and typically tiered in sequence of study from basic to advanced studies. However, the smallest circle, nonformal education, focuses on a topic of immediate application, a targeted learning delivered by a targeted means.

What kind of education does the church need? Which one should it utilize? Practicing Christian education calls us to use all three forms of education. Practicing Christian education at its best intentionally makes use of all three to promote the formation of faith. Also, some educational initiatives can combine

Figure 1.1
Educational Contexts and Learning

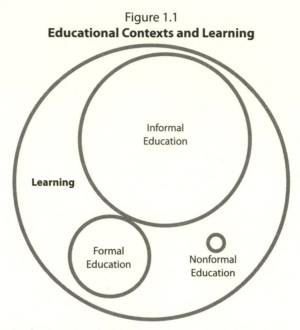

Based on George R. Knight, *Philosophy and Education: An Introduction in Christian Perspective* (Berrien Springs, MI: Andrews University Press, 1998), fig. 2.

for maximum effectiveness. Consider your Christian college or seminary experience. It is a formal learning environment, but learning also occurs through supervised ministry experiences/internships (nonformal), as well as learning from the campus ethos and relationships formed (informal). Church camp is more nonformal, with a focus on immediate application and short duration, but is also indeed informal in its learning. When participating in the life of the congregation, we are learning through socialization (informal education); but when we get involved in serving within the congregation, we are often trained through a seminar or workshop (nonformal education). Practicing education in the church involves formal, nonformal, and informal learning.

Why Do We Need *Christian* Education?

George Gallup and Jim Castelli conclude, "Americans revere the Bible but, by and large, they don't read it. And because they don't read it, they have become a nation of biblical illiterates."[4] Stephen Prothero affirms the continuing presence of religion, particularly Christianity, in American culture and Western civilization. However, he raises an alarm regarding Americans' virtual ignorance of religious content, even among those who are active participants in an organized religion. Who is to blame for this failure of religious literacy? As many evangelicals charge, in this instance the removal of religion from the public school curriculum is one of the main culprits. However, Prothero readily identifies a second culprit: *Christian education*! He notes that churches themselves have failed to instruct their members in their faith's basic tenets.[5]

Ignorance of the Bible's content among everyday Americans is even more pronounced. Only 50 percent of adults in the United States can provide the title of one Gospel, and most cannot recall the first book of the Bible.[6] Barna Group has made some disturbing revelations about Americans' grasp of Bible content and their changing perception of the Bible:[7]

- 60 percent of Americans cannot name even five of the Ten Commandments
- 82 percent of Americans believe "God helps those who help themselves" is a Bible verse
- 12 percent of adults believe that Joan of Arc was Noah's wife
- Over 50 percent of graduating high school seniors thought that Sodom and Gomorrah were husband and wife
- A large number of respondents to one survey indicated that the Sermon on the Mount was in fact preached by Billy Graham
- Four out of ten believe that the same spiritual truths are simply expressed differently in the Bible, the Qur'an, and the Book of Mormon

The church faces a devastating twofold problem: a simultaneously expanding and shrinking gap between it and the culture. First, the gap between the church and culture is *expanding* due to society's ever-increasing ignorance of biblical content, which poses a significant challenge to the church. Second, unfortunately, the gap is likewise *shrinking* because the church is also becoming less knowledgeable about the Bible and significant matters of faith. *Not* practicing Christian education is *not* a viable option. It endangers our mission not only to "go . . . make disciples" but also to teach them (Matt. 28:19–20). We cannot expect people to have a vibrant faith, nor the church's health and vitality to be advanced, in the absence of an intentional, holistic approach to practicing Christian education.

What's the Point?

Education is not just Sunday school; it is bigger than that. Also, education may be more complicated than commonly thought. Likewise, education is serious ministry for Christian educators. Christian education forms an environment wherein believers are instructed, equipped, and nurtured for a life of faith in the real world.

Reflection Questions

1. How would you describe an *educated* Christian in a church context?
2. How would you define or describe *education* in your church?
3. In your congregation, where does formal, nonformal, and informal education occur?
4. How would you explain the value of Christian education in two or three sentences?

Suggestion for Further Reading

Mayr, Marlene. *Does the Church Really Want Religious Education?* Birmingham, AL: Religious Education Press, 1998.

Biblical Principles for
Practicing Christian Education

The Bible is not a theology textbook, nor is it a God-given "user guide for life," as if it were all arranged systematically and sequentially, with an alphabetic index. Essentially, the Bible is a story. A true story, but nonetheless it is a story, laid out in narrative, expounded on in poetry, reflected upon in epistles; it is the story of God's people from the time of creation to the birth of the church to the consummation of creation. However, it is not just a story for story's sake, or for its entertainment value; rather, it is a story with a unique purpose. As Romans states, "For whatever was written in former days was written for our instruction, that through endurance and through the encouragement of the Scriptures we might have hope" (15:4). This story was given to teach us. Notice Paul's affirmation of the practical nature of the God-breathed story: "All Scripture is breathed out by God *and profitable* for teaching, for reproof, for correction, and for training in righteousness, that the man of God may be complete, equipped for every good work" (2 Tim. 3:16–17, emphasis added). Scripture isn't just any story; it is God's story given by God to his people, the church, and part of the story is about teachers, teaching, learning, places of learning, and reflections on what we need to know. For Christian educators, as we endeavor to be "equipped for every good work," the Scriptures play an integral, irreplaceable role for practicing Christian education. The Bible gives us insight into the educational practices of God's people throughout its story, from which principles for today's Christian educator can be gleaned.

The Bible Explains *Why* We Are Practicing Christian Education

Why education that is Christian? Educating God's people is a fulfillment of God's divine imperative to teach. Why do we teach? Because God commanded it in his story. The Old and New Testaments are replete with examples of the commitment of God's people—faithful men and women, families, communities, congregations, and nations who were dedicated to fulfilling God's call to teach others. For most of us, the divine mandate might be sufficient, but it still begs the question, Why did God command us to teach?

Teaching God's story is a catalyst for conversion and the formation of a distinctively Christian faith. Biblical instruction's purpose is the formation of the individual and the community with a distinctively Christian faith. A holistic Christian faith is the vital objective of Christian education. Without Scripture, conversion and faith are generic rather than focused on the God who revealed/inspired the Word and redeemed/transformed the individual. This is why teaching the Scriptures, particularly in the Old Testament, included foreigners who were living among the Hebrews (e.g., Deut. 31:12; 1 Kings 8:41–43). Scripture is relevant to our spiritual lives before conversion, during conversion, and throughout our walk with Christ.

The earliest educational mandate given by Moses expresses the essential nature of godly instruction for faith formation, especially for children, in Deuteronomy 6:4–9. After affirming the essential theology of the Hebrew community (vv. 5–6), Moses then identifies the means by which the community will transfer its faith to the next generation (vv. 7–9). Many of Judah's national spiritual revivals were predicated on the teaching of God's Word. Jehoshaphat (eighth century BC) sent court officials, Levites, and priests "to teach in the cities of Judah. . . . And they taught in Judah, having the Book of the Law of the LORD with them. They went about through all the cities of Judah and taught among the people" (2 Chron. 17:7, 9). Centuries later the catalyst of Josiah's sixth-century-BC revival was the people's "hearing all the words of the Book of the Covenant that had been found in the house of the LORD. And the king stood in his place and made a covenant before the LORD, to walk after the LORD and to keep his commandments and his testimonies and his statutes, with all his heart and all his soul, to perform the words of the covenant that were written in this book," to which they were faithful all the days of his life (2 Chron. 34:30–31).

In the New Testament, Jesus's Great Commission isn't *just* about evangelism ("Go"); it's also about making disciples ("teaching them"; Matt. 28:19–20). Christian education—the ministry of teaching—not only responds to the mandate of Jesus to teach, the command of the Great Commission, but also sustains the rationale that it is vital for the faith formation of the believer. This is true for not only the individual but the group as well. Luke summarizes the earliest Christian community as having "devoted themselves *to the apostles' teaching* and fellowship, to the breaking of bread and the prayers" (Acts 2:42, emphasis added). Christian education facilitates the formation not only of personal faith but also of a faithful community of believers.

The Bible Itself Is Formative in Our Students' Lives When We Practice Christian Education

While the Bible is not the only source of spiritual nurture, it is indeed given to us as a formative element in our walk with Christ. The lyric to a simple child's song, "Jesus loves me, this I know, *for the Bible tells me so*," sums up the matter. Without the Bible, we could not know who Jesus is, properly experience his love, or do what he wants us to do. We can proclaim WWJD (What Would Jesus Do?), but we can really do this only once we know WDJD (What Did Jesus Do?). Biblically speaking, learning and teaching are inseparable. Nothing bears this out more than the fact that in Hebrew *lamad* means "to teach" and is in the active voice, while "to learn" is in the passive voice. The concept of teaching/learning is indivisible—two sides of the same coin.

Scripture's formative influence on our lives is not only for the mind but for the whole person. When instructing Timothy about dealing with the false teachers in Ephesus in 2 Timothy 3:14–17, Paul urges him to be different from them: "But as for you . . ." (v. 14). But how? He tells Timothy to think differently from them, to be "acquainted with the sacred writings, which are able to make you wise for salvation" (v. 15). Paul then affirms the divine authority of Scripture ("All Scripture is breathed out by God" [v. 16a]) and the practical nature of Scripture for life transformation ("profitable for teaching, for reproof, for correction, and for training in righteousness" [v. 16b]). Why is this crucial? "That the man of God may be complete, equipped for every good work" (v. 17). The Bible is foundational to practicing Christian education because it is formative for our minds, our lives, and our vocation. Remember the impossibility posed by John Stackhouse? "Christians are somehow expected to think and feel and live in a distinctive way, as followers of Jesus, without being provided the basic vocabulary, grammar, and concepts of the Christian religion."[1]

The Bible Even Tells Us *How* It Is to Be Used
in Practicing Christian Education

Lecture? Object lessons? Storytelling? Streaming video? No single teaching method is prescribed or described as the sole method of instruction in the Bible. Scripture presents a continuum of teaching/learning methods designed to meet the needs of the individual and the situation. This spectrum extends from the more teacher-centered, fixed content for indoctrination to the more student-centered, process-oriented method of instruction, such as Job or Ecclesiastes.[2] In fact, perhaps the only restriction about how the Bible is to be taught isn't methodological, but is the instruction found in 2 Timothy 2:15: "Do your best to present yourself to God as one approved, a worker who has no need to be ashamed, *rightly handling the word of truth*" (emphasis added). The integrity of the content is always to be affirmed, regardless of our chosen teaching method.

The diversity of teaching methods is evident throughout the Old Testament, such as in the teaching methods of the prophets.[3] It is definitely demonstrated in the book of Proverbs alone, wherein the vocabulary for teaching/learning ranges from the more passive, teacher-centered learning methods (listening, obedience, observance, assimilation) to the more active, student-centered approaches (understanding, mastery, searching, pondering).[4] This same continuum is in the New Testament as well. The vocabulary used in it to describe learning reflects methods ranging from the more teacher-centered, content-oriented approaches (e.g., "instruction," Eph. 6:4; "instructed," Acts 18:25; "instruction," 1 Cor. 10:11) to those that seek the deeper levels of learning beyond the mastery of content (e.g., "understand," Eph. 5:17). Perhaps the most distinct portrait of the variety of teaching methods employed in the New Testament is in Luke 24. Jesus's encounter with disciples on Emmaus Road includes discussion (v. 14), probative questions (v. 17), challenging ideas (vv. 25–27), modeling learning objectives (vv. 30–31), and direct instruction (vv. 33–35).

The Bible Identifies Who Is Supposed
to Be Practicing Christian Education

Teachers have always existed within the community of faith, taking a diversity of forms, titles, and roles among God's people in both the Old and New Testaments. Perhaps the only teachers common to both testaments are God (Isa. 3:8; Job 36:22; Exod. 35:34; Titus 2:11–12; 2 Cor. 6:1; 1 Tim. 2:3–4) and the faith community. God instructs primarily through his acts of grace and revelation, teaching through word and deed. While often unacknowledged, the faith community itself also serves as a teacher. For example, in the Old Testament, the festivals, placement of worship sights, and activities of public assemblies all had educational implications (Deut. 4:14; 6:1; 26:1–19; 31:39; Josh. 8:30–35; 2 Kings 2:3; 4:38; 5:22; 2 Chron. 17:7–19). In the New Testament, participation in the church reinforced the formation of faith through exposure and involvement in the community (Acts 2:42–47). Additionally, the place and function of the teacher is valued as a gift from God (Rom. 12:3–8; 1 Cor. 12:27–31; Eph. 4:7–13, 29–32; 5:15–20; 1 Pet. 4:10–11).

However, within the people of God some individuals have been committed to the teaching ministry. In the Old Testament, the *family* had primarily educational responsibilities for its children (Exod. 12:26–27; 20:4–12; Deut. 4:9–10; 6:6–7; 11:19–20; 29:9; Ps. 78:3–6; Prov. 1:8; 6:20) and was even intergenerational (Deut. 4:9–10; 11:19–20; Exod. 12:26–27; Ps. 78:3–6). Early in Israel's history the *prophets* arose (Jer. 8:8; 9:13; 16:11; Mic. 6:8; Isa. 8:3–16; 42:21–24; Zech. 7:12; Hos. 1:3–9)—starting with Moses, who was the exemplar for all future prophets (Exod. 18:20; 24:12; Deut. 4:14; 6:1; 31:19)—as well as the *priests* (Deut. 22; Pss. 27:31; 40:8; Hag. 2:11; Mal. 2:6–9; 3:11). Other groups assumed instructional roles in Israel, such as the *sages* (Judg. 14:12–14; 2 Sam. 13:1–22; Prov. 3:3–11; 10:8; 12:15; 13:14; 14:2; 28:4–9) and, later in Israel and Judah's history, the *scribes* (Neh. 8; Jer. 8:8; Ezra 7:10–11).

In the New Testament, in addition to God and the faith community, the apostles became the initial teachers. As Jesus's former students, they assumed the task of teaching through instructing, preaching, and writing. Acts depicts the apostles as completing Jesus's mission (Acts 1:1) by making disciples for Christ (Acts 14:21). Doctrine assumes a crucial role in the church through the apostles' instruction (Acts 2:42; 5:28; 13:2; 17:19). As the church expanded, both numerically and geographically, pastors and teachers were selected for newly planted congregations. Teaching is a vital facet of leadership in the church. The ability to teach is an essential quality of leadership (1 Tim. 3:2; Titus 1:9). Paul further affirmed that the church should let "the elders who rule well be considered worthy of double honor, especially those who labor in preaching and teaching" (1 Tim. 5:17). However, the Bible does more than just tell us that teachers teach. Practicing Christian education requires us to know the kind of person who can teach the people of God.

Perhaps the most stellar example of a teacher within the community of faith is Ezra. He was in exile in Babylon, one of many Jews who found themselves in Babylon following the destruction of Jerusalem in 586 BC. However, he was given the daunting task of restoring the faith of God's people upon their return to Judah around 428 BC. Scripture states, "For Ezra had set his heart to study the Law of the LORD, and to do it and to teach his statutes and rules in Israel" (Ezra 7:10). This verse provides a glimpse into the kind of person suited to be a teacher in God's Kingdom. First, Ezra was a devotee: he "had set his heart." We can make the application here that teachers have a heart condition, a motivated conviction that is not determined by externals. They are reliant on God, love students, and serve in the church.

Second, Ezra was a student of God's Word: "to study the Law of the LORD." In Ezra 7 he is described several times as a scribe who was learned in the Scriptures, so much so that his learning even commanded the Persian king Artaxerxes's respect (7:6, 11, 21). A Christian teacher must be one who knows God's Word as well as one who is capable of "rightly handling the word of truth" (2 Tim. 2:15c). Good teachers start out as good students.

But, third, Ezra was also a disciple: "and to do it." It is not enough to know the Word. Teachers must apply it to their own lives—practice it—before they stand before others and teach it. In regard to practicing our faith, the book of James states, "But be doers of the word, and not hearers only, deceiving yourselves" (1:22). The experience of discipleship is crucial for teachers, since without it they may be accused of hypocrisy; and yet with it they can readily identify with the struggles of faithfully living for Christ and provide practical advice from their own walk.

Finally, Ezra was a teacher: "to teach his statutes and rules in Israel." Teachers have to teach, and Ezra taught the people. Nehemiah 8 gives an ample description of Ezra as a teacher, as one who publically read and expounded from the Book of the Law, "from early morning until midday, in the presence of the men and the women and those who could understand. And the ears of all the people were attentive to the Book of the Law" (Neh. 8:3). Education isn't an impersonal activity; it requires teachers.

The Bible Describes the Occasions When We Are to Practice Christian Education

Christian education doesn't take place just in a classroom, on Sunday morning, scheduled so as not to interfere with the worship service. This notion, while common, is too restrictive and obstructs the potential for instruction in the church. Previously we discussed the teachers in the Bible and the wide span of educational venues in which they taught, guided, trained, and discipled believers; so it should be clear that Christian education can occur anywhere, from a dungeon to a palace, and anytime, whether in the afternoon at an

Ephesian school borrowed by the apostle Paul (Acts 19:9), in conversation on a road to a nearby city (Luke 24), or through everyday life encounters in the home (Deut. 6:6–9). Scripture does not impose when or where education can or cannot take place; but it does implore us to teach others, to pass along our faith when given any opportunity.

The people of God introduced new means of education, adapted the practices of other cultures, and even removed obsolete means as deemed necessary. The Hebrews, as a people, grew from being a family to an ethnic group, a tribal nation, a monarchy, and eventually an exilic people group with some returning to reclaim their nation. These changes shaped the way in which they educated; the institutions of education had to adapt to the people's changing needs. For example, the rise of the monarchy was a catalyst for the formation of royal court education, scribal schools, and the production of Wisdom literature. However, with the collapse of the monarchy, the first two of these went away, with only Wisdom literature remaining. The exile and return of the sixth to fifth centuries BC served as yet another catalyst for the birth of an educational venue unmentioned in the Old Testament yet frequently encountered in the New Testament—the synagogue. When you major in Christian education you're not majoring in Sunday school, or small groups, or weekly Bible studies; the Bible affirms a wide array of educational opportunities presented for God's people.

Conclusion

Why are we even concerned with biblical foundations for Christian education? Ultimately, the response to this question lies in the very affirmation of Scripture as the revealed and inspired Word of God (1 Cor. 2:10–13; Rom. 3:1–3; 2 Tim. 3:15–17; 1 Pet. 1:10–12, 21; 2 Pet. 1:20–21; 3:2, 15–16). As believers in Jesus Christ, we make the same affirmations Jesus made regarding Scripture (Matt. 5:18; 22:29; Mark 7:8–9; 12:24; John 17:17), affirming its trustworthiness and truthfulness. The Bible is the cornerstone of our own faith and the faith of the church, the primary textbook for all of us.

Reflection Questions

1. How would you describe your own use of the Bible, personally and in ministry?

2. In your spiritual walk, how has the Bible been a catalyst for your formation as a Christian?

3. Given the biblical foundations, how have you perhaps limited or minimized your understanding of Christian education?

4. How would you summarize this entire chapter in one paragraph?

5. Given the description of Ezra as a devotee, student, disciple, and teacher, how would you rate yourself in these facets of your ministry? What could you do to improve on them?

Suggestions for Further Reading

Crenshaw, J. A. *Education in Ancient Israel*. New York: Doubleday, 1998.

Estep, James Riley, Jr. "Biblical Foundations for Christian Education." In *Evangelical Dictionary of Christian Education*, edited by Michael J. Anthony, 82–85. Grand Rapids: Baker Academic, 2001.

———. "Biblical Principles for a Theology for Christian Education." In *A Theology for Christian Education*, edited by James Riley Estep Jr., Gregg R. Allison, and Michael Anthony, 44–72. Nashville: B&H, 2008.

———. "Philosophers, Scribes, Rhetors . . . and Paul? The Educational Background of the New Testament." *Christian Education Journal* 2, no. 1 (2005): 30–47.

Zuck, Roy B. *Teaching as Jesus Taught*. Grand Rapids: Baker, 1995.

———. *Teaching as Paul Taught*. Grand Rapids: Baker, 1998.

Theology for Practicing Christian Education

Most people have a theology. They have presuppositions and beliefs about God. These beliefs are often shaped from personal experiences or formed from their faith heritage. In many of these cases their beliefs about God—or their theology—are not well informed. They have not studied theology in a formal context. Studying theology is never to be viewed as an abstract exercise in gaining information; rather, theology is very practical. Theology provides the processes to ensure that our teaching, preaching, and ministry remain faithful to the gospel. Theology not only is the content of Christian education but also shapes and molds the life of the Christian educator and the assumptions that inform education that is Christian; it even shapes the practicing of Christian education. In fact, theology actually tells Christian education what it is *supposed* to be doing.

Our understanding of theology—what we believe about God—plays an important role in shaping our faith and our view of Christian education. What we believe about the Triune God (Father, Son, and Spirit), human persons, sin, redemption, the church, and the end times influences the practice of Christian education. This chapter provides an overview of the primary theological doctrines and their relationship to Christian education.

Revelation

Theology is the study of God. It is the "queen of the sciences." We study God in order to gain an understanding of how God reveals himself to humanity. We

admit that it is impossible to fully understand the revelation of God, but we
have been given significant sources to understand God. One of the ways the
Triune God reveals himself to us is through God's revelation. God reveals to
humanity both through *specific revelation* (the Bible) and *general revelation*
(creation). We study the Bible and creation as a means to explore truth because
we believe that in these two sources we can find all truth.

One of the primary resources in understanding God is the Bible. We read
and study the Bible in order to understand how God relates to his people. We
believe that the Bible is divinely inspired or "breathed out by God" (2 Tim.
3:16) and provides all that is necessary for our understanding of salvation.
The Bible is a book that was inspired by God and conveyed through humans.
In other words, God speaks through the Bible, and theology is the response of
intellectual attentiveness and moral obedience that God's Scripture demands
and deserves.[1]

God also reveals himself through *general revelation*, or *natural theology*.
We learn about God through creation. As we gaze on a beautiful sunset or
receive a wet kiss from our dog, we are reminded that God is speaking to us.
This is why it is important for us to understand how God made humans and
the created world. We study all disciplines, including psychology, sociology,
biology, science, and the humanities, because they provide a greater understanding of God's nature. For example, the social sciences are an investigation
of God's created order and can aid in our understanding of general revelation.

We believe that in Christian education we must understand God's truth
through both specific and general revelation. Our understanding of the sciences
and theology informs the content and methods of Christian education. We
believe that both specific and general revelation reveal God's truth, and that
"all truth is God's truth." In other words, we do not see a conflict between what
God has revealed in Scripture and what we learn from the sciences, because
both testify to the nature of God (see chap. 5). Practicing Christian education
calls us to embrace all of God's truth in its entirety, regardless of the source.

Theological Methodology

There are varying interpretations of the content of the Bible. Some view the
Bible primarily as a source of propositional knowledge—a book of facts
that is often disconnected from real life. Others view the Bible as a book of
historical accounts that can be separated from contemporary life. Although
each of these has merit, we believe that the primary content of the Bible is
the *narrative or story* of God. This narrative leads the readers to understand

the nature of God and what God has done *to* and *with* humanity. Since Scripture is a narrative, it doesn't provide answers to all of life's questions. It is not a sourcebook or cookbook with recipes, but instead is a story of God's redemptive history.

Christians approach the Bible in a variety of ways. Each Christian denomination interprets the Bible and applies it to faith in a particular way. All of them are seeking to understand God's truth as revealed in Scripture. Everyone interprets the Bible through a set of lenses shaped by their experiences and their particular church denomination or tradition.

One approach to theological understanding, attributed to Albert C. Outler, is called the *quadrilateral*.[2] He developed this view from the theology of John Wesley, the founder of Methodism. The quadrilateral is a theological methodology to determine whether something is true theologically or doctrinally. It consists of the following sources: Scripture, tradition, reason, and experience. The quadrilateral provides significant insights into biblical interpretation. The following is a brief summary of each source of the quadrilateral.

Scripture: Wesley was a man of one book—the Bible—and believed that Scripture was the primary source. He followed the Reformers' view of *sola Scriptura* (Scripture alone) by placing the authority of Scripture above the other sources.

Tradition: In referring to tradition, Wesley believed that we should look to the early church fathers in the development of doctrines and beliefs. Tradition provides a basis to see how Scripture has been interpreted through the centuries.

Reason: When interpreting Scripture, it is important to use human reason in making decisions about theology and doctrine. This doesn't mean that you can reason yourself to God, but it does mean that you should think critically and question the Bible.

Experience: It is important for people to experience their faith and to confirm that experience with Scripture.[3]

Christian educators view the Bible as the primary content of teaching; therefore it is important to interpret Scripture appropriately. As Christian educators lead Bible studies, preach, and teach, it becomes important to utilize the quadrilateral as a framework to properly handle "the word of truth" (2 Tim. 2:15). As the Holy Spirit guides us, we can properly understand God's specific revelation to help others grow in their relationship with God. Practicing Christian education is an interpersonal activity between the teacher, student, and the God-given Word.

Triune God

One of the primary doctrines of the Christian church is that God is one essence and three persons, or *hypostases*—the Father, the Son (Jesus Christ), and the Holy Spirit as one God in three persons. These three persons are distinct and of one nature. So when speaking about God, we must first begin with understanding the Triune God.

The Triune God is in relationship with Godself. Many scholars believe that the three persons of the Trinity are in a *perichoresis*, or "circle dance." This is referred to as a *social trinitarian view*. Within this circle dance, God communes with Godself, bringing a sense of joy, freedom, and intimacy to the relationship. This relational approach to the Triune God provides a model for a relational approach to Christian education, one that centers on the interconnectedness of humans and all of creation. In this sense, God is *immanent* and thereby engages in relationship with his creation. The relationality (*immanence*) and the holiness (*transcendence*) of God are simultaneously at work. God is holy and exhibits a holiness that is radically different from humanity. God is transcendent as a wholly other God. God's relationality models perfect love. The three members of the Godhead are in perfect relationship and express holy love toward one another. This means that God's relational love toward humanity extends out of the very being of the Trinity. While the Trinity describes the essence of God, aspects of the Triune God give insight into the nature of God's character.

God the Father

God is the First Person of the Trinity and is our heavenly Father. As Father, God is distinctive within the Trinity. God as Father is a metaphor to describe God's relationship to humanity in a personal way. Just as a human father is to care for and love his children, so God the Father is concerned about caring for and loving his creation. God is holy love and remains loving to all of creation. God offers love for humanity and desires communion with creation.

God created all of creation out of nothing (ex nihilo), which shows that the world's existence emerges from a gracious God. God also created humanity in his image and likeness (*imago Dei*). Because they are created in God's image, humans have a special and privileged place in God's creation. This special relationship between God and humanity was not completely severed by the fall of humanity. As Christian educators, we must recognize that our students are created in God's image and that we are to value them and recognize that God is working in their lives.

God as Creator is a reminder that God continues to create and make things new. As humans engage in God's redemptive work in the world, both humans and creation are being restored and redeemed. For Christian educators, this is a reminder that God is creating through our faithful teaching. It also shows us that education is more than transmitting information; it is also fostering students' ongoing creative imagination.

In understanding the character of God, the following attributes have been used to describe how God relates to the world.

- Omniscience: God knows all things
- Omnipresence: God is present everywhere
- Omnipotence: God is all-powerful
- Goodness: God is good
- Immutability: God is changeless
- Sovereignty: God is over all creation
- Justice: God works for good
- Holiness: God is pure and loving
- Righteousness: God is just and good

What we understand about the character of God influences our theological foundations of Christian education. For example, since we believe that God is holy, the goal of education is that we embody a life of holiness, by God's grace, and that through our modeling and teaching, others would embody the same life. In other words, our goal in Christian education is, by the grace of God, to help persons live a life of faithful discipleship.

Jesus Christ

The Second Person of the Trinity is Jesus Christ. The study of Jesus Christ is called *Christology*. Jesus was born of the Virgin Mary and consisted of both humanity and divinity. We refer to his birth as the *incarnation*. His *atonement* reflects what he did for all of humanity and creation. It is through the life, death, burial, and resurrection of Jesus that we have the opportunity to be forgiven for our sins. He modeled for us self-giving love expressed through a life of service and death on the cross. This is best expressed in the *kenosis* (emptying) hymn of Philippians 2:1–11. Jesus "emptied" himself of power and became a "servant" or "slave" (*doulos*, v. 7). He became human and dwelled among us, taking the form of a slave.

Jesus is the God-man. He is both human and divine. Throughout the history of the church, theologians have sometimes placed a greater emphasis on either his humanity or his divinity. In either case, Jesus is both fully God and fully man.

Holy Spirit

The Holy Spirit is the Third Person of the Trinity. The theology of the Holy Spirit is called *pneumatology* (*pneuma* means "breath"). Jesus promised that after he ascended into heaven he would send an advocate or helper (John 14:15–31). John says in verse 26, "but the Helper, the Holy Spirit, whom the Father will send in my name, he will teach you all things and bring to your remembrance all that I have said to you." The Holy Spirit represents the personal activity of God and Jesus Christ in the world today. It is through the work of the Holy Spirit that persons are convicted of faith and drawn to God. When a person is converted they are born again of the Spirit.

The power of the Holy Spirit enables Christians to live as faithful disciples. Christians are able to embody the "fruit of the Spirit" (Gal. 5:22–23) by the work of the Holy Spirit. The Holy Spirit works in the context of the body of Christ to bring about unity in the body (Eph. 4:3) and to enable the body of Christ to utilize its gifts (1 Cor. 12:1).

The ministry of the Holy Spirit includes direct activity with human persons in the life of the church and in the world. The Holy Spirit enables humanity to bring about the redemption and restoration of all creation.

Anthropology (Doctrine of Humanity)

God created male and female in his image and likeness (*imago Dei*; Gen. 1:26–27). God created humans to be in relationship with him and with each other. We are social beings who desire companionship. God created humans to have a unique relationship with him and to be God's ambassadors on earth. Because we are created in the image of God, we represent God.

But through the sin of Adam and Eve, our first parents, humans became fallen. This means that humans broke relationship with God by their disobedience. Some theological traditions refer to this fallenness as total depravity, a condition in which the image of God is completely destroyed and humans do not have the capacity to respond to God. Other traditions (including the authors') believe that the image of God was distorted and yet humans have the capacity to respond to God. This means that there is still goodness in all of humanity. We, the authors, also believe that one of the primary goals of salvation is the full renewal of the image of God, which reflects Christlikeness. This is possible only by God's grace and the work of the Holy Spirit.

Because of the fall of our first parents, sin is inherited from them. Every person is in a state of sin and needs the redeeming work of Christ in their life. Sin is to be understood in relational terms, as a breach between humans and God and between one another. Sin negatively affects a person's relationship with God, with others, with oneself, and with the earth. It is through holy love that sin is cured.

As Christian educators, we are to recognize that since all persons are created in the image of God, they have the capacity to grow, learn, and develop. This means we need to respect all persons and to value them as God's creation. It also means our role is to partner with God in their redemption by loving them and providing accountability. Humans are social beings created for relationships. Practicing Christian education is indeed a relational ministry, whether it is with children, adolescents, or adults, with new believers or old believers. The educational avenues we provide for social interaction and fellowship are important.

Soteriology (Doctrine of Salvation)

Since humans are fallen, we need to be redeemed and restored to the image and likeness of God. This can take place only by the saving grace of Jesus Christ. The study of salvation is called *soteriology*. We believe that we are saved by God's grace because of the death of Jesus Christ. His self-giving love expressed through his life, death, burial, and resurrection provides the means for us to live holy lives. When we ask God to forgive our sins, we are justified and adopted into the family of God. This is called *justification*. This is forensic/judicial language to convey that Christ saves us from the guilt of sin and restores us in God's favor. We are also made new creatures in Christ (2 Cor. 5:17), or regenerated. Through regeneration we are changed and transformed, or made new in Christ. We are adopted into the family of God, which means we have been saved from separation from God. We now have a restored relationship with God and with other Christians.

Once we are justified by faith, we grow in God's grace as we move toward a holy life, or *sanctification*. Sanctification is the ongoing process by which we are being conformed to the image of God (Christlikeness). Sanctification is a deeper commitment to love God and neighbor fully. To be a sanctified person is to be *set apart* or *made holy* through spiritual growth in Christlikeness by the indwelling power of the Holy Spirit. It requires our faithful and obedient response to God's grace in our lives, which helps us grow toward maturity in faith. In this regard, we are empowered by the Holy Spirit to live out God's mission in the world by loving God and others.

Ecclesiology (Doctrine of the Church)

The study of the church is called *ecclesiology*. The Greek word *ekklesia* means "congregation" or "the assembled." A variety of terms are used to describe the church: "the people of God," "the body of Christ," or "the fellowship." What is the primary purpose of the church? Why should we attend a local church? Can we be Christians without a connection to the local church? These are important questions about the purpose of the church.

There are three primary purposes of the church. First, the church is a place where believers gather to grow spiritually through their relationships with each other. This takes place through small groups, fellowship, and being present to each other. The church is a healing community, a place of love, acceptance, and hospitality. As people engage in close relationship with each other, there are opportunities for confession, healing, and community. Second, the church is where we worship God, hear the gospel, and receive the sacraments. It is through the Word (preaching) and the Table (Communion) that believers are challenged and empowered to live out God's mission in the world. For most churches, the preaching of the gospel is central to worship, while for other churches, the proclamation of the gospel includes both Word and Table. Some denominations practice Communion weekly, while others practice it less frequently. In either case, Communion provides not only a remembrance of Christ's life and death but also healing and spiritual growth for believers. Third, the church is missionally engaged in the world, offering hospitality, justice, and the proclamation of the Kingdom of God. As the church gathers for worship and its members are present to each other, it provides what we need to be God's witnesses in the world.[4]

Christian educators play a significant role in helping to nurture faith in the church through small groups, worship, and mission. The Christian educator can work to ensure that the practices that take place in church reflect its primary purposes. Practicing Christian education isn't just about classrooms, lecterns, and content; it's also about acts of worship, praise, and devotion.

Eschatology (Doctrine of End Times)

The study of the end times is called *eschatology*; the word *eschaton* means "last" or "end." Eschatology has to do with the hope in Christ and the end of

God's story. *The end times* has three important theological meanings. First, *end times* refers to a timetable of events that mark the end of the world as we know it. The end is marked by the second coming of Christ, the resurrection of the dead, and the final judgment. In other words, eschatology reminds us that the universe as a whole and our individual lives are limited.

The second meaning of eschatology is probably more significant because it focuses on God's goal for the end of creation. In other words, what do we believe God's intentions are with creating the world, and where will it all end up? As we read in Revelation 22, God the Creator will create the world anew. God will bring about a new heaven and a new earth. All things will be redeemed and restored.

Third, closely associated with the second meaning of eschatology, is that God has a vision of shalom. We find ourselves between the first coming of Christ and the second coming of Christ, in the "already/not yet" Kingdom of God. In this sense, the Kingdom of God is present through the coming of Jesus Christ and through God's continual working through Christians by the Holy Spirit. But the fullness of the Kingdom is not realized until the end. Therefore, eschatology includes our participation with God's mission in the world to bring about the healing of creation, or shalom. As we engage in God's mission in the world, we bring the Kingdom of God today. This is why we work to see the Kingdom come today, but we look with great hope for the final coming of the Kingdom of God.[5]

As Christian educators we must teach these meanings of eschatology and provide an educational opportunity to engage in God's redemptive work today. This can include mission trips, engagement with justice issues, compassion ministry, caring for the elderly, and a variety of service projects.

Theology and Practicing Christian Education

There are a variety of approaches to understanding how theology relates to Christian education.[6] We believe that theology provides the primary *content* for Christian education, that theology is a *reflective process* that deepens our relationship with God, and that theology is an *integrated practice* with Christian education. Practicing Christian education requires us to explore each of these.

1. *Theology as content*: We agree with those who believe that Christian education serves as a vehicle of theological doctrine. This means that theology is the primary content, and Christian education provides the

processes and methods to communicate the content. The goal of this approach is not to transmit information as much as it is to see persons grow and develop in Christlikeness.

2. *Theology as a reflective process*: We believe that Christian education serves not only as a vehicle of theological doctrine but also as a reflective process that deepens our understanding of God. For example, what we believe about the Triune God affects how we understand our relationship to God and to others. In other words, our understanding of the Triune God helps us grow in our relationship with God and others. The goal in understanding theology is that it provides an informed approach to our Christian lives.

3. *Theology as an integrated practice*: We believe that theology and Christian education are integrated. The integration of the social sciences (general revelation) with theology (specific revelation) provides the basis for Christian education to be Christian. In essence we believe that theology and the social sciences are complementary with the goal of Christian education.

It is important that the Christian educator understand these important relationships between theology and Christian education, as they help the church live out its mission to develop faithful disciples of Jesus Christ.

Conclusion

What we believe about God impacts our relationship with God and others. Theology is not an end in itself; rather, it is a process that helps us deepen our relationship with Christ. In other words, theology informs how we practice our faith. Our understanding of God's revelation as both general and specific provides a basis for our understanding that "all truth is God's truth." We can see the complementary relationship between Scripture and the social sciences and how it applies to Christian education. Our understanding of a theology of the church that includes believers gathering for fellowship, hearing the Word proclaimed, and participating in the holy sacrament of Communion affects how we educate in the context of the church. And ultimately, it affects how we engage in God's redemptive mission in the world.

It is important for the Christian educator to properly understand theology, since it is the source of teaching and instruction, and to properly understand how theology and the social sciences are integrated. With this proper understanding of theology, the Christian educator can provide the necessary foundation to help others grow in Christlikeness.

Reflection Questions

1. Why study theology? Why do Christian educators need to understand the doctrines of the church?
2. How do both specific and general revelation affect our understanding of Christian education?
3. What can we learn about relationships from our understanding of the doctrine of the Trinity?
4. What are the primary purposes of the church? What is the Christian educator's role in ensuring that these purposes are being achieved?
5. What are the various meanings of eschatology? What are the practical implications of eschatology for Christian educators?

Suggestions for Further Reading

Estep, James Riley, Jr., Michael J. Anthony, and Greg R. Allison, eds. *A Theology for Christian Education*. Nashville: B&H, 2008.

Johnson, Timothy L. *The Creed: What Christians Believe and Why It Matters*. New York: Doubleday, 2003.

Lodahl, Michael. *The Story of God: A Narrative Theology*. Kansas City, MO: Beacon Hill, 2008.

McGrath, Alister E. *Christian Theology: An Introduction*. 3rd ed. Oxford: Blackwell, 2001.

Seymour, Jack, and Donald E. Miller, eds. *Theological Approaches to Christian Education*. Nashville: Abingdon, 1990.

The History of Practicing Christian Education

What can possibly be practical about history? How can the history of Christian education help us do Christian education today? Simply put, there were Christian educators practicing Christian education for centuries before we existed. Failing to take into account their contributions to Christian education is professional and pastoral myopia, never seeing beyond the short length of our own life, basing our ministry only on what we have experienced without any long-term appreciation for the giants on whose shoulders we now stand. We are the successors of our forerunners' work; what they accomplished or failed to accomplish continues to influence us today. With an appreciation for history, we may be able to identify an apparently amazing innovation as in fact a modernized ancient practice.

We never escape the hold of history. The decisions, theologies, educational theories, learning institutions, social movements, and ministry innovations of the past provide the foundation on which contemporary Christian education ministry is built. For example, the "modern" small group movement, typically dated to the late 1970s, actually doesn't date back to the biblical practices of the ancient church. The "small groups" in the New Testament existed out of necessity. Since Christianity was under suspicion and persecution for the

---

This chapter is based in part on James Riley Estep Jr., ed., *C.E.: The Heritage of Christian Education* (Joplin, MO: College Press, 2003), introduction, chap. 1, and chap. 16 (the latter by Jonathan H. Kim). Mark A. Maddix was also a significant contributor to *C.E.* as our first writing collaboration.

first four centuries of its existence, the church existed in small groups. That is hardly the contemporary model of small groups. However, John Wesley did develop a system of small groups that formed the congregation into societies (midsized groups), classes (small groups), and bands (accountability groups). The "modern" small group movement is simply a reinvention of a ministry model that is literally centuries old, recontextualized for twentieth- or twenty-first-century American culture, but the principles and some practices are almost identical. This is the practical value of Christian education's history. It brings into focus the principles and practices of today's church by appropriating for us the broader and deeper perspective that only the heritage of Christian education can bring.

Dominoes in the History of Practicing Christian Education

Consider this: history is like dominoes. Each piece represents a period of history, each with its contributors to education. Like a line of dominoes, one falling into the next, creating a chain reaction, history is a progression of one generation of educational innovators influencing the next over the centuries. For example, today's Sunday school, a common feature of children's ministry, was not a twenty-first-century invention, or twentieth or nineteenth, but was the conception of Robert Raikes in Gloucester, England, in 1780. However, the Raikes Sunday school would be unrecognizable compared to today's version, having gone through five major reconfigurations over more than two centuries.[1] By understanding the heritage of Sunday school, or any Christian education ministry, we can learn from our predecessors and begin to learn from their thoughts and ideas on education. However, the total history of Christian education is a domino line about four thousand years old, extending back into Old Testament history.

Tables 4.1 and 4.2 summarize the precursors to Christian education, the antecedents to it, and then the development of Christian education from the time of Christ to today. They are by no means comprehensive and they focus strictly on Christian education and its contributors throughout time. While theories, practices, ideals, and models beyond the Christian community did interact with Christian education, the scope and focus of this chapter will not allow for a more thorough treatment (see the suggested readings at the end of the chapter for more comprehensive treatments of Christian education's history).

Christian education was not born in a vacuum, written on a blank slate, created ex nihilo. No. Rather, the items in table 4.1 serve as the environment

Table 4.1 Precursors to Christian Education

Period	Dates	Major Contributors	Significant Development in Christian Education
Early Hebrew	2300–1050 BC	• Moses • Priests • Early prophets	• Socialization through living in Hebrew community • Instruction through family, home, and tribe • *Torah* in Hebrew means "instruction," a curriculum for Hebrew living • Core of Hebrew education is the basic confession, the Shema • Tabernacle as instructional institution • Rise of the Hebrew monarchy
Later Hebrew	1050–586 BC	• Sages • Wise men • Latter prophets	• Royal court instruction • Scribal schools to support the monarchy • Temple as instructional institution • Rise of Hebrew Wisdom literature • Fall of the Hebrew monarchy
Jewish/Judaism	586 BC to present	• Scribes, e.g., Ezra • Rabbis—Pharisees • Ben Sira (third century BC) • Simeon ben Shetah (second century BC)	• Exile in Mesopotamia (i.e., Babylon and Persia) • Rise of the synagogue (i.e., local Jewish worship and instruction sites) • Jewish elementary schools (*Beth Hassepher*) • Jewish secondary schools (*Beth ha-Midrash*) • Rabbinical academies, for the training of rabbis (*Beth ha-Midrash* or *Beth ha-Talmud*) • Completion of the Old Testament canonization • Codifying the oral traditions (i.e., Midrash, Mishnah, and Talmud)

Greek or Hellenistic	Eighth century BC to first century AD	• Homer (eighth century BC)
		• Sophists (fifth century BC)
		• Socrates (469–399 BC)
		• Plato (427–347 BC)
		• Aristotle (384–322 BC)
		• Isocrates (436–338 BC)
			• Class-based education
			• Education for character development, in service of the state
			• Instruction given by three schools:
			  • *Grammatist* (reading, writing, and letters)
			  • *Kitharistes* (music, poetry, and literature)
			  • *Paedeotribe* (physical education, gymnastics, and athletics)
			• Formation of the Trivium and Quadrivium—the seven liberal arts
			• Rise of Hellenistic universities in the fourth and third centuries BC
			• *Pedagogos* was a family slave responsible for tutoring and instruction of students
			• Library of Alexandria established in Egypt (translation of Old Testament into Greek [Septuagint] was done here)
			• Eventually integrated with and replaced by Roman education

continued

Period	Dates	Major Contributors	Significant Development in Christian Education
Roman Education	First century BC to fourth century AD	• Cicero (106–43 BC) • Quintilian (AD 35–95) • Plutarch (AD 50–120)	• Roman education was heavily influenced by Greek theory and practice until the first century AD, when it grew increasingly independent of Greece • Purpose of education was the *vir bonus*—the "good man" • *Humanitas*—the "humanities" are the core curriculum • *Pedagogue* was the Roman adaptation of the Greek *pedagogos* • Paralleling the Greek model, the Romans developed three levels of school: *ludus* (elementary), *schola* (secondary), and higher education (rhetorical instruction)

in which it was formed. It by nature was essentially an extension of Jewish education, with Jesus and Paul as its primary voices. However, as Christianity grew beyond Judea, into the Greek and Roman world of the Mediterranean, the influences of Greco-Roman education began to shape the formation of Christian education (e.g., the use and redefinition of educational terms in the New Testament).[2] The early church began to adapt the basic elements, institutions, practices, and curriculum in its educational endeavors, facilitating a distinctively Christian education in the Roman world that soon became the dominant religious ideal in Europe, the Middle East, and North Africa. Table 4.2 describes the rise of Christian education.

Lessons from Our Christian Education Ancestors

What have we learned about the history of Christian education? What factors have shaped it in the past that may still play an influential role in its future? Here's a partial list of the major factors shaping Christian education then and now.

Theology (Philosophy)

Theology and education are inseparable. Theological shifts in the church have an almost automatic response in Christian education as a means of presenting and promoting the new theological development. Luther's Reformation was as much educational as theological, since he needed an educational system that would undergird and support his theological reforms. The four major theological shifts in the twentieth century had immediate implications for education in the church in terms of outcomes, content, and even instructional methodology. Macro-themes in theology, let alone some of the more minor points, tend to shape Christian education, often without notice. Our theology forms assumptions about pastoral ministry and Christian education that often go unnoticed but are nonetheless present.

Technological Advances

We often think of technology as part of the digital revolution that started in the 1980s. But technological advancements have challenged educators

Table 4.2 Rise of Christian Education

Major Christian Education Contributors	Significant Developments in Christian Education
Early Christian—First to fifth centuries AD	

• Jesus and Paul (first century)
• Clement of Alexandria (150–216)
• Origen (185–254)
• Cyril of Jerusalem (315–87)
• Augustine of Hippo (354–430)
	• Christian education begins in a Jewish context
	• By mid-first century AD it begins reflecting some Greco-Roman influence (e.g., vocabulary of the New Testament)
	• Balance of *kerygma* and *didache*—preaching of the good news and instruction
	• Early Christian communities in the late second century begin establishing Christian schools, adapting the Roman *ludus* for their use
	• Two forms of Christian education schools emerge:
	  • Catechumenal—instruction in practical Christian living
	  • Catechetical—instruction in formal academic subjects, especially theology and philosophy
	• Two main questions that shaped Christian education: Should Christians study the writings of Greek and Roman authors? Should Christians send their child to a Roman school?

Medieval Education—Fifth to fourteenth centuries	
• Benedict of Nursia (480–543) • Alcuin (735–804) • Anselm of Canterbury (1034–1109) • Thomas Aquinas (1224–74)	• Christian education is its own fusion of Christian theology with the influence of Greco-Roman tradition (humanities) and practices (schools) • Rise of monastic schools (fifth century), with two forms—residential (*schola claustra*) and nonresidential (*schola canonica*); theology and the humanities • Episcopal/cathedral schools (twelfth century) for pastoral and lay training, and very elementary education for children • Early European universities were in fact Christian—i.e., *Univeritas* ("one truth") • Scholasticism dominated the latter medieval era, integrated intellect with spirituality

continued

with the choice to either reject or accept them for much longer. For example, Socrates, the fifth-century-BC Greek philosopher, rejected the most revolutionary technology of his era, considering the alphabet to be a threat to education since it threatened to undo the prevailing practice of memorization as the basis of learning. Considered the most influential historical development of 1000–2000, the invention of the printing press revolutionized Western culture, causing the first information explosion, challenging Christian education with the availability of resources and printed materials, not to mention Bibles, in the vernacular. It seems that those who adopt

Major Christian Education Contributors	Significant Developments in Christian Education
Renaissance Education—Fourteenth to sixteenth centuries	
• Francisco Petrarch (1304–74) • Vittorino da Feltre (1378–1446) • Gerhard Groote (1340–84) • Desiderius Erasmus (1466–1536) • Juan Luis Vives (1492–1540)	• Northern Renaissance was more religious, centered on theological instruction • Southern Renaissance was more secular, breaking from purely theological instruction • Two forms of modern university emerge from the two foci of the Renaissance • Private and public schools begin to emerge in major European cities, but with little success • The humanities were retained in the core curriculum • Groote forms the Brethren of Common Life, best schools in this period for providing instruction to anyone capable of participating • Vives promoted an inductive curriculum vs. the standard deductive curriculum—i.e., more student centered
Reformation and Education—Sixteenth century to 1650	
• Martin Luther (1483–1546) • Philip Melanchthon (1497–1560) • John Calvin (1509–64) • Ulrich Zwingli (1485–1531) • John Knox (ca. 1505–72) • Ignatius of Loyola (1491–1556) • Francis Xavier (1506–52)	• Three actual Reformations occur in sixteenth-century Europe: • Luther advocated a state-sponsored public education with the church in support • Calvin advocated a church-sponsored education, with the state in support • Jesuits favored education sponsored by the church-state, regarding the two as integrated • Education was principally done the same way as in medieval and Renaissance practices • Focus on literacy due to affirmation of "priesthood of believers" and Scripture being translated into their own vernacular • Advocacy for publicly funded, universal education in their own vernacular; the formation of public libraries • Jesuit *Ratio Studiorum* was a comprehensive fifteen-year curriculum for training scholars

continued

Major Christian Education Contributors	Significant Developments in Christian Education
Enlightenment and Christian Education in Europe—1650 to nineteenth century	
• John Amos Comenius (1592–1670) • John Locke (1632–1704) • Phillip Jacob Spener (1635–1705) • August Hermann Franke (1663–1727) • Nikolaus Ludwig von Zinzendorf (1700–1760) • Robert Raikes (1736–1811) • John Wesley (1703–91)	• Christian education begins to grow distinct from the more secular European education • The public funding of schools is a more popular ideal, with Christian educators serving as primary supporters • Common schools—vocational, elementary education • Grammar schools—instruction in humanities in Greek and Latin • Focus on early childhood education • Human nature is a tabula rasa (blank slate) rather than depraved from birth • Pietist movement begins in Germany and moves throughout Europe, with a focus on the devotional study of Scripture in small groups • Sunday school addresses the social concern for educating impoverished children • Small groups emerge in spiritual movements as a primary means for Christian education • The prototype of modern Christian schools begins to emerge in Europe (e.g., the Kingswood School in Bristol)
Early America—Seventeenth to nineteenth centuries	
• Horace Bushnell (1802–76) • Horace Mann—promoter of public education in United States, but marginally religious (1796–1859) • Alexander Campbell (1788–1866) • George Scofield (church libraries—1810–87)	• American education was for piety, morality, and utility (in that order), but by the twentieth century only utility remained • Colonies and eventually states provided for public education in a variety of ways, but always with the support of the church; especially for the less fortunate • Puritan public schools of New England were innately Christian (e.g., established schools through the "Old Deluder Satan Act" [1642 and 1647]) • Sunday schools were established in the colonies by 1737, and in the United States grew into local, regional, and even national Sunday school unions and conventions to promote and support their advancement • All higher education institutions, except the University of Pennsylvania, were started by various denominational groups • Bushnell's *Christian Nurture* (1846) is undeniably the most controversial spiritual formation and education book of the nineteenth century in the United States, challenging Puritan tradition • The Bible college movement began in the late nineteenth century as a means of rapidly equipping pastors in response to the growing secularization of American universities • Church library movement in United States (1789)

continued

Christian Education in the Twentieth Century—1900–2000

Christian education in the twentieth century "fragmented" into four distinct camps, based on theological divisions, and hence for clarity the chart has to change.

1. *Classical liberal religious education* (early twentieth century)
   - Tied to the rise and fall of the classical liberal theological movement
   - George Albert Coe (1862–1951) and Harrison S. Elliot (1882–1951)
   - Religious Education Association and *Religious Education* (journal)
2. *Neo-orthodox religious education* (mid-twentieth century)
   - Tied to the rise and fall of Karl Barth's neo-orthodox theological movement, which declined sharply in the late twentieth century
   - Sara Little (1919–2009) and Randolph Crump Miller (1910–2002)
3. *Resurgence of evangelical Christian education* (latter half of twentieth century)
   - Tied to the rise of evangelical theology following World War II
   - Kenneth O. Gangel (1935–2009) and Frank E. Gaebelein (1899–1983)
   - National Association of Evangelicals and National Sunday School Association
   - Society of Professors in Christian Education and *Christian Education Journal*
4. *Specialized theological forms of education* (late twentieth century)
   - Liberation, feminist, homosexual, ethnic, or social-science approaches
   - James Michael Lee (1931–2004)

Early Twenty-First Century (So Far)—2001–

Perhaps this is the point of the entire chapter: we're still writing the chart. You, reading this right now, are part of the present, but soon, in a decade or two, will be part of history. What will be your educational legacy that you pass on to the next generation of Christian educators?

and apply newly developed technologies stay ahead in Christian educational ministry.

Societal Context

Christian education was born not in a vacuum but within a society and culture that shaped it. Christian educators too are shaped by their personal histories, which are inextricably tied to their chronology and geography. Likewise, Christian education is often used as a response to a social or cultural challenge. Robert Raikes's response to the needs of poverty-stricken families, and particularly children, gave rise to the formation of the Sunday school. It was a direct response to the situation in which Raikes found himself. Similarly, the resurgence of evangelical education after World War II was a direct result of individuals seeing the plight of the world as in part due to the fall of evangelical beliefs around the world and hence seeking to reverse that fall.

Concept of Human Learning and Development

The scientific study of psychology and sociology, especially in regard to human development and learning, was new during the seventeenth century. For example, John Amos Comenius wrote his *Orbis Pictus* as a revolutionary new idea, the children's book, in part due to his realization that children could in fact learn at a very early age, especially when shown pictures of items. Hence, because of this newly uncovered idea about learning, with its equally new way of teaching, he was given the title "father of modern education," Christian or otherwise.

Relationship of the Church to the Culture

In colonial New England, schools were operated by the church in the Puritan manner. Even when students learned the alphabet, it was "A is for Adam, B is for Bible . . ." The teachers had not only professional credentials but personal religious ones as well. In fact, so Christian were the schools of New England that the Sunday school was virtually nonexistent there. The church and culture were so intertwined, so inseparable, that the Sunday school was seen as an unnecessary redundancy. On the other hand, in the early church, Tertullian (third century) advocated that no Christian child be sent to a public Roman *ludus* (school) because there was nothing in common between Roman culture and Christian belief. The church's relationship with the culture indeed does shape Christian education.

Advances in Knowledge

We have periodically experienced information explosions, which typically facilitate an educational paradigm shift. The fourth-century-BC Greek philosopher Aristotle's request that his pupil Alexander the Great supply him with specimens for his zoo and botanical garden as well as rocks for his geology lab caused an information explosion in the West. Centuries later, the discovery of the New World by Columbus produced a very similar voluminous increase in available knowledge. Likewise, the printing press, mentioned earlier, allowed the dissemination of information to be more rapid and affordable, as well as allowing the production of textbooks and academic journals. Now, in the twenty-first century, the internet, although it is decades old, still manages to facilitate an information explosion for our generation, with the world literally being at our fingertips. What will Christian education do? How will it ride the wave of the new information surge?

Condition of the Family

Regardless of the educational endeavors the church may launch, they are all only auxiliary to the family's influence on the education of children and adolescents. The synagogue was formed by the Jews as a means of preserving their faith in foreign lands, as well as providing a faith-friendly alternative to formal instruction that was based on the family. In fact, all forms of education, from the ancient world to today, regard the parents as essential to the educational success of their children. Similarly, Christian education has always been part of the church's responses to life needs among its members, including those going through family stress and strain.

Personal Life of the Educator

We are only human. All the previous factors mentioned here do not just influence Christian education but do so through the mind, heart, and faith of the Christian educator. The legacies of Christian education before us are the results of men and women of faith over the last millennia. History is biography. For example, think of your convictions and values about Christian education. They are formed by your own personal experiences in your home church, including the experiences facilitated through church camp, vacation Bible school, youth groups, and so on. You were shaped by your own personal history with your own Christian community, and that will influence you personally and pastorally. Now, back out of the picture to the theological traditions of the twentieth century that shaped that congregation, and you begin to see the broader influences that shaped your experience, and so on all the way back to Jesus and Paul.

Conclusion

In your ministry, do you plan to keep a journal of some kind? Perhaps collect pictures of events, people, the church buildings, or images of those with whom you serve? Do it. It's part of your personal history. It will bring strength, encouragement, and motivation for the decades of service to come. The same could be said about this chapter. It is designed to be the album, the journal, of the personal history of the contributors to Christian education and the developments they fostered. From it, you can gain insight, encouragement, and cautions, but most importantly a view forward. When you drive a car, you need to look forward. But isn't it curious that most cars have three mirrors pointing back, to what you've already passed—to the past? Before moving forward, changing lanes, or slowing down, we check our mirrors to gain our position. We are not living in the past, just looking back in order to look forward to the future and our part in forming the next domino in the chain.

Reflection Questions

1. Before reading this chapter, what was your level of appreciation for the history of Christian education? What is it now? Did it change? Why?
2. What factors influenced your own personal history of encountering Christian education? How has it shaped your convictions and calling to Christian education?
3. What do you think will be your contribution to the work of Christian education? What do you hope to accomplish?

Suggestions for Further Reading

Anthony, M., and W. S. Benson. *Exploring the History and Philosophy of Christian Education: Principles for the 21st Century*. Grand Rapids: Kregel, 2003.

Burgess, Harold W. *Models of Religious Education*. Wheaton: Victor Books, 1996.

Elias, J. L. *A History of Christian Education: Protestant, Catholic, and Orthodox Perspectives*. Malabar, FL: Krieger, 2002.

Estep, James Riley, Jr., ed. *C.E.: The Heritage of Christian Education*. Joplin, MO: College Press, 2003.

Reed, J. E., and R. Prevost. *A History of Christian Education*. Nashville: Broadman & Holman, 1998.

Wyckoff, D. Campbell. "Theology and Education in the Twentieth Century." *Christian Education Journal* 15, no. 3 (1995): 12–26.

Education as Christian

"If someone wants to be a Christian educator, why don't they major in education at a state university and then study the Bible and theology in seminary?" Is that really it? Is the Christian part of education in the church just about the content? Is education so value-neutral that *any* approach to education is acceptable for use in the church? No, education that is Christian is far more than this. It is a matter of not just function, practice, or pragmatics but defining the very substance of education as Christian. It is ensuring that Christian education is both soundly Christian and a valid form of education; not one or the other, not a separate set of concerns, but one concern for a genuine education that is innately Christian.

Christian education is actually a practical theology, or as D. Campbell Wyckoff defines it: "Christian education is a theological discipline that draws upon the behavioral sciences."[1] Similarly, Jack L. Seymour observes that "theology is more than the content of Christian education; it is a process of instruction and discernment by which persons are educated in their identity, interpret the realities of their lives, and are sent into the world. . . . [This is] the task and vocation of practical theologians of education."[2] Education that is Christian is the result of the dynamic interaction between theology (biblical, systematic, confessional, etc.) and the social sciences (learning theories, human development theories, etc.), fused into a consistent approach to education in the church. But what is that relationship like? How do the parts interact and fuse?

Approaches to Theology and Education[3]

Not everyone expresses the *Christian* in education in the same way. Likewise, not everyone defines *education* that is Christian in the same way. At a very foundational level, it depends on the way one assesses the relationship between theology and the social sciences in producing a distinctively Christian education. Essentially, three approaches are often used by educators in the church to express this issue:

- Exclusivity approach: theology versus social sciences
- Primacy approach: theology over social science or social science over theology
- Integrative approach: theology and social sciences in dialogue

Exclusivity Approach

Wouldn't it just be easier to use either the social sciences or theology? Why bother with using both? It is an either/or approach, and a neither/nor as well. The exclusivity approach rejects the necessity of either the social sciences or theology, regarding one or the other as totally sufficient for forming a theory of Christian education. However, in their extreme opposition, pitting the validity of one over the other, advocates of this approach do not realize that they commit the same grievous error regardless of which one they select. For example, if a Christian educator were to use a purely scientifically derived approach to Christian education or formation, then, as Romney Moseley observes, "Christian education would be criticized for confusing the goals of the Christian formation of persons with those psychological theories of human development."[4] If one were to affirm the social sciences' exhaustive sufficiency to form a theory of education in the church, what would make it Christian? Such an approach may well be present in public schools or state universities, but once again, would it make the term *Christian* anything more than a functionary title rather than having real substance?

However, before anyone opts for an exclusively theologically based Christian education, with no regard for the social sciences, realize that it is no more valid than the social-science exclusivity position. While somewhat more palatable to Christians, because it seems to support scriptural sufficiency (cf. 2 Pet. 1:3; Mark 12:24; 1 Cor. 2:13–16; Luke 11:28; 16:27–31; James 1:25; Heb. 4:12; Ps. 19:7–11),[5] sufficiency does not mean that the Bible is the exhaustive knowledge of all God's revelation, as it does not include that given through creation, and certainly the Bible was never meant to convey that the exhaustive knowledge of truth is contained within creation. Where in the Bible can we learn the best teaching methods to use with seven-year-olds? Or how the cognitive function of a child differs from an adolescent? Neither Scripture nor theology provides that kind of specific information.

The simple assessment is this: the exclusivity position is insufficient. Without the social sciences, Christian education is just theology; but without theology, Christian education is just practices based on the social sciences, with nothing distinctively Christian about it. Perhaps even more importantly, to hold the exclusivity position, one has to either deny the authority and relevance of God's first revelation, creation, or do the exact same to God's special revelation, the Word. Perhaps the challenge before us is best stated by the late Dr. Ted Ward: "Christian education is *neither*. . . . In far too many cases Christian education is neither thoroughly Christian nor soundly educational."[6] We need both theology and the social sciences to genuinely form an education that is substantially Christian.

Primacy and Integrative Approaches

Rather than choosing *either/or*, these approaches are *both/and*. Both the primacy approach and the integrative approach are actually degrees or methods of integrating the social sciences and theology, but on what basis can a Christian educator explain why this is actually necessary? Why bother trying to use both theology and the social sciences? Three factors explain why integration is critical: (1) God as the Author/Creator, (2) the unity of truth, and (3) the necessity of human inquiry. Scripture affirms that God reveals himself both through his special revelation of Scripture (2 Tim. 3:16; 2 Pet. 1:20–21) and through his general revelation of creation (Job 38:1; Rom. 1:18–22; chap. 3). Like David in Psalm 19, integrationists affirm, "The heavens declare the glory of God, and the sky above proclaims his handiwork. Day to day pours out speech, and night to night reveals knowledge" (vv. 1–2), and they equally assert, "The law of the LORD is perfect, reviving the soul; the testimony of the LORD is sure, making wise the simple; the precepts of the LORD are right, rejoicing the heart; the commandment of the LORD is pure, enlightening the eyes" (vv. 7–8). This affirms that "all truth is God's truth," regardless of its sources; truth is a singular truth, not plural truths. Our inquiry into creation and Scripture is the means by which social science discoveries and theological assertions, *both* critical, in their own way, form a sufficient basis for Christian education (see also chap. 3). Figure 5.1 illustrates the basis of the primacy and integrative approaches.[7]

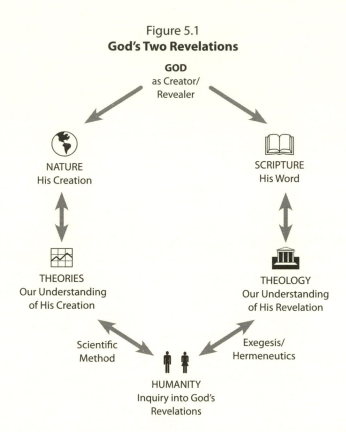

Figure 5.1
God's Two Revelations

Figure 5.1 illustrates that God is the source, the Author, of all truth, and that truth has been revealed by him through both nature (creation) and Scripture (the Word). They are the means by which we have received God's truth. We seek his truth by inquiring into his revelations. *Science* is the methodology and means by which humanity studies God's creation, resulting in the formation of theories that capture God's revealed truth about the physical universe. *Exegesis* and *hermeneutics* are the means and methods by which humanity studies the Word, God's special revelation, resulting in the formation of theologies that endeavor to process and systematize God's truth. While God's revelations—the Word and creation—are sources of his unified truth, it is our fallible human means and methods of inquiring into that truth from which contradictions and inconsistencies emerge. Our inquiries are *not* equal to God's revelation but are mere reflections of it. To neglect either the social sciences or theology is to commit the error of the exclusivist approach, rejecting the insights gleaned from one of God's revelations. The question is: How do the social sciences and theology interact, relate, and form a distinctively *Christian* education?

An Illustration[8]

These three basic integrative options can be illustrated by how a student approaches writing a term paper on a Christian educator's understanding of human development. The student has a book on Paul's theology of humanity, as exemplified by any number of theological traditions, and Jean Piaget's *The Psychology of the Child* (1966),[9] signifying the social sciences. How does that student integrate them? How does that student write about the question of human development?

- *Exclusivist approach*: The student uses either Piaget or Paul, unaware of the other's relevance or value to the subject, choosing to simply use one rather than both. The paper is a summary of the insights on human development from either the social sciences or theology, depending on which the student selects.

- *Primacy approach*: The student, while using both Paul and Piaget, nevertheless places a priority of relevance and value on one over the other, using the other in a supporting role. The student could grant prevalence to the social sciences and use theology in support (i.e., social science primacy), or grant prevalence to theology and use the social sciences in support (i.e., theological primacy). Hence, one forms the substance while the other is used as the veneer or just provides embellishment. The paper is primarily based on the social sciences or theology, with the other used sparingly or as illustration.

- *Integrative approach*: The student uses Paul and Piaget in concert to form a jointly derived understanding of human development, based on both theology and the social sciences. Both form the substance of the paper, being valued as equally valid and insightful for use in Christian education. This approach possesses the advantages of the previous approaches, without their limits or shortfalls. Hence, the paper is the result of the integration of theology and the social sciences.

The fullest expression of Christian education is one that is consistent and holistic in its use of the social sciences and theology, not as opposing sources but as complementary uses of God's revelation of nature and his special revelation in Scripture. It is the product of affirming and utilizing the truth revealed through God's revelations of creation and Scripture so that it becomes a comprehensive and cohesive approach to education that is distinctly Christian.

Figure 5.2
Student Integrative Endeavor

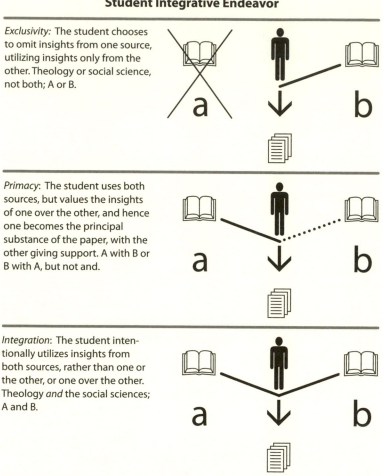

Exclusivity: The student chooses to omit insights from one source, utilizing insights only from the other. Theology or social science, not both; A or B.

Primacy: The student uses both sources, but values the insights of one over the other, and hence one becomes the principal substance of the paper, with the other giving support. A with B or B with A, but not and.

Integration: The student intentionally utilizes insights from both sources, rather than one or the other, or one over the other. Theology *and* the social sciences; A and B.

Christian Education *Is* Integration

At the opening of this chapter we said that Christian education is the result of the integration of theology and the social sciences. But what kind of integration? Placing Christian education into the broader context of faith/learning integration brings this matter to a point of clarity, enabling it to aid us in practicing Christian education. While multiple models of faith/learning integration exist, perhaps the model most conducive to practicing Christian education is the one presented by Kenneth Badley.[10] In the context of his concept of faith/learning integration, *faith* can be defined as either Christian living or Christian theology, and *learning* can mean either the process or content of learning; or as Badley labels it, *faith* is "life of faith" and/or "body of doctrine," and *learning* is "process of learning" and/or "body of knowledge."[11] Figure 5.3 captures his model.

Figure 5.3
Badley's Faith/Learning Integration Model

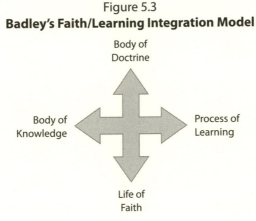

Body of
Doctrine

Body of
Knowledge

Process of
Learning

Life of
Faith

While most depictions of faith/learning integration are satisfied with the integration of the academic (i.e., theology, academic disciplines) and the process/procedures of either (e.g., hermeneutics or research design), Badley adds the practical, essential, but often obscured element of Christian living. He affirms that faith is more than intellectual assent or the content of our beliefs; it includes the life we live. This addition of Christian living as a valid dimension of faith in the faith/learning integration agenda enables it to apply beyond the classroom, discipline, or academic dimension of Christian education and enter the personal, pastoral, and actual practicing ministry.

Using Badley's paradigm of *faith* and *learning*, Christian education *itself* is the product of just such an integrative process, as illustrated in figure 5.4. Christian education is the integration of a body of knowledge (educational theories) and the body of doctrine (Christian theology); but it does not stop there. The integrative process likewise includes the process of learning (social sciences' research design and theology's hermeneutic) as well as the life of faith (Christian formation).

Christian education is not *only* theology, or *just* an educational theory, nor solely concerned with social science research, and not even equivalent to Christian formation. *It's all four.* In fact, it's all four and then some, given that the synergy between them results in an entirely new thing that is more than the sum of its parts: Christian education.

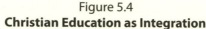

Figure 5.4
Christian Education as Integration

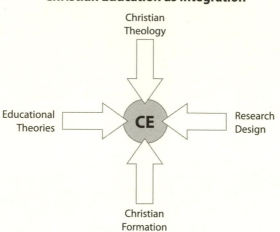

The Christian educator must become a student of all four disciplines, not just one. Education that is Christian is a theological discipline with insights from the social sciences, realized through the teaching ministry of the church, for the formation of mature Christians, all integrated and informed by the theological convictions of the faith community. Hence, when we do Christian education, the Christian educator must be a theorist, one who has a distinctive approach to education that is suited and relevant for the church. The educator must be a teacher, one who can engage in the primary expression of the educational task, along with the pastoral and administrative responsibilities required by the ministry. They must be a trainer, one who can guide, direct, and nurture the Christian formation of believers through a lifelong relationship with Jesus Christ. Ultimately, the Christian educator must be a theologian, which is the framework that unites all these elements into one cohesive ministry.

Reflection Questions

1. What could you do to better integrate your theological convictions with your work as a Christian educator?
2. What is the relationship between theology and the social sciences? How does it apply to the practice of Christian education?

3. What presents the greatest challenge to thinking simultaneously theologically and educationally about your ministry?

Suggestions for Further Reading

Estep, James Riley, Jr. "Developmental Theories: Foe, Friend, or Folly?" In *Christian Formation: Integrating Theology and Human Development*, edited by James Riley Estep Jr. and Jonathan H. Kim, 37–62. Nashville: B&H, 2010.

———. "What Makes Education Christian?" In *A Theology for Christian Education*, edited by James Riley Estep Jr., Gregg R. Allison, and Michael Anthony, 25–43. Nashville: B&H, 2008.

Gaebelein, Frank E. *The Pattern of God's Truth: The Integration of Faith and Learning*. Winona Lake, IN: BMH Books, 1985.

Harris, Robert A. *The Integration of Faith and Learning: A World View Approach*. Eugene, OR: Wipf and Stock, 2004.

6

Christian Education as Ministry

It is easy to confuse Christian education with schooling, or being a teacher, or even working in a university. Christian education can be practiced in a Christian school, and it does indeed involve teaching, and even now you may be sitting in a Christian college, university, or seminary reading this book. But defining Christian education by where it is practiced or by what specific tasks it is associated with misses the fundamental point. *Christian education is ministry.*

Ministry is not reserved for those who are in the pulpit or who serve on Sunday mornings in the auditorium or sanctuary. Ministry is also done in the classroom, in small groups, and standing behind a lectern. But what is ministry, and what is unique about practicing education as ministry?

What Is Ministry?

The word *ministry* in the New Testament is actually a translation of two different Greek words, which might be a place to start but not the place to finish. *Diakonia* simply means "service" and is a very general term translated numerous ways, including "ministry." A more specific term translated "ministry" is *leitourgia*. It refers to a special function of priests in the old covenant (Luke 1:23; Heb. 8:6; 9:21).[1] However, as the church is a priesthood of believers (2 Pet. 2:5–10), we shouldn't be surprised that the word in the New Testament is not limited to a Levitical priesthood but is used to affirm the ministry of believers who constitute the church (Phil. 2:7, 30; 2 Cor. 9:12).

Is that it? Ministry is *service* done by Christians? Yes, but it is much more. It is not just a matter of the basic meaning of these terms, but how they are used in Scripture to present a portrait of ministry. Several conclusions about ministry and the minister can be drawn.

First, ministry is what God does *for* people *through* people. Paul, when writing to the Corinthians, reminded them of the reconciliation they had received in Christ, saying, "All this is from God, who through Christ reconciled us to himself *and gave us the ministry of reconciliation*; that is, in Christ God was reconciling the world to himself, not counting their trespasses against them, and *entrusting to us the message of reconciliation*. Therefore, we are ambassadors for Christ, *God making his appeal through us*. We implore you on behalf of Christ, be reconciled to God" (2 Cor. 5:18–20, emphasis added). As ministers, we are servants on behalf of God to his people. In the New Testament, Christians minister to Jews, gentiles, and fellow believers (Acts 21:19; Rom. 11:13; 2 Cor. 9:1; Gal. 2:8). This ministry of reconciliation represents the triumph of the Spirit and grace over sin and the law (2 Cor. 3:7–9), as Paul summarizes: "For the letter kills, but the Spirit gives life" (2 Cor. 3:6).

As Christian educators, we can never lose sight of the people. In the midst of programs, organizational charts, calendars, and special events, it is easy to lose focus and forget about those to whom we are supposed to minister. We serve people through the education ministry of the church, which is committed to the transformation of individuals to the likeness of Christ—Christian formation.

Second, ministry is both a general and a personal service by the people of God. Yes, the church collectively ministers to those within and without (Acts 6:1; 11:29; Rom. 12:7; 1 Cor. 12:5). God's people minister in the community in which they live and within the congregation to one another. However, ministry is also tied to specific functions within the church, in which an individual may have a special sense of call to ministry. For example, the apostles were called to a specific kind of ministry (Acts 1:25; Rom. 11:13; Gal. 2:8). It is also tied to specific individuals called by God to do specific service (Eph. 4:12; 2 Tim. 4:5, 11). Our call may not be to preach, or to direct worship, or even to plant churches; but the call to teach and minister through the education ministry of the church is no less personal and valuable than these.

Third, ministry requires a *call* from God. The New Testament authors use the imagery of *receiving* the ministry from God, as if it were in fact a gift (Acts 20:24; 2 Cor. 4:1; Col. 4:17). Quantifying the sense of calling is almost impossible. It is more than a checklist of qualifications; rather God seems to first *summon* an individual to the task of ministry, and even if resistant at first, the individual eventually *desires* to serve in accordance with God's will. For example, leaders in the church must serve "not under compulsion, but willingly, as God would have you" (1 Pet. 5:2), and if a Christian "aspires to the office of overseer, he desires a noble task" (1 Tim. 3:1). Remember, people's initial reaction to God's calling is not always affirming, since it seems to expose their inadequacies for the task. Moses has sudden timidity (Exod. 3:2–6), Jonah just runs in the opposite direction from his call (Jon. 1:1–3), Isaiah and Peter have a sudden confession of unrighteousness (Isa. 6:4–5; Luke 5:4–8), the prophet Jeremiah is frustrated (Jer. 20:9–10), and the prophet Amos is reluctant (Amos 7:14–15). In fact, sometimes we are so resistant that God has to resort to extreme measures, such as bringing a zealous Pharisee to the ground without sight (Acts 9:1–9) to become the most effective missionary of all time—the apostle Paul. Hopefully no one reading this book will be this resistant to God's call.

Finally, the message of ministry is the Word of God (Acts 6:4), and most specifically the gospel (Rom. 15:19). Regardless of whether we stand behind the pulpit or beside a lectern, our words are not our own. We minister to people on behalf of God, who placed a call on our lives and has now given to us the ministry of reconciliation through Christ. We learn of Christ's work (the gospel) through God's Word, which he has delivered to us. Christian educators practice their ministry by sharing, studying, discussing, and presenting the Word of God to those who do not know it or need to know it more intimately and profoundly.

Defining Marks of a Christian Education Pastor

Just as practicing Christian education is different than practicing other ministries of the church, serving as a Christian education pastor likewise is distinct from other pastoral roles. These distinctions not only clarify our calling into a ministry of Christian education but also give direction to our preparations for a career. You need not have all these indicators, but the more you have, the more certain that your calling is to Christian education.

- *Lectern, not pulpit*: While there is more to serving as a lead pastor than preaching, preaching is the primary "public" work of a lead pastor. For the Christian educator, it is not the pulpit that has appeal but the lectern. Rather than the larger setting, it is the classroom or small group that is more attractive. One seems suited more to teaching than preaching. While the two are indeed related, and the relationship has been debated for some time, they remain distinct in content, audience, setting, and outcome. Regardless, the Christian educator seems more drawn toward the lectern than the pulpit.

- *Trees, groves, and the forest*: Christian educators tend to view the church somewhat differently than other ministers on staff. While for some the primary venue for the congregation is the forest (worship service, large group gatherings), for the Christian educator, the venues are smaller, focusing on the small or medium-size groups (trees and groves) constituting the church. One of the distinctive marks of the Christian educator is that they see the church as a compilation of groups of varying sizes, ages, and other designations rather than principally as the whole. Christian educators deal with the parts rather than the whole, the trees rather than the forest.

- *Beyond worship*: For many, the health, vitality, and growth of a congregation is gauged by the church's worship attendance. "How many people do you have in your church?" typically is answered by "We have about 450 in worship." However, the Christian educator sees beyond the worship head count and assesses the health of the congregation by the number of cells constituting the body and the strength and vitality of ministries within the church; they want to move beyond the mere number of those in worship service toward a deeper, more substantial figure about the congregation's vitality. It is not just attendance and participation in the celebration service that matter; it is how many are studying, learning, growing, building relationships, developing skills, and serving others within the church as a whole. Christian educators typically see beyond the worship service as their ministry context and focus.

- *Age/niche defined*: Unlike many other ministries in the church, Christian education ministries often have a distinction of age or a specialized niche. Prenatal ministry, early childhood ministry, children's ministry, youth ministry, adult ministry, and seniors ministry are all Christian education. They have the distinction of being age-related ministries, often called *generational* or *next-gen* ministries, or even *intergenerational* ministries; regardless, the point is that they are indeed defined by age. Another distinction is niche, such as men's ministry, women's ministry, parents' ministry, or some other form of ministry that is based on a niche population of the congregation or community. If this is how you are practicing ministry, then you are probably practicing Christian education.

- *Administration*: While all ministries require a degree of administrative attention and effort, the Christian education minister spends a significant

amount of time doing administrative tasks or working with an administrative team. In fact, administration is one of the principal means of
ministry for the Christian educator, since it involves training, equipping,
resourcing, planning, organizing, and leading others toward fulfilling
the mission, vision, and strategy of the church. If you have some draw
toward administrative tasks, then you might be well suited for a Christian education ministry.

- *Ranchers all*: A classic distinction in ministry philosophy is shepherd
  versus rancher. While a variety of nuances have come about from the
  original dialogue, the basic comparison is that shepherds tend to work
  directly with the sheep, being solo leaders who assume responsibility
  for all the work of the ministry. On the other hand, ranchers work
  with and through others, developing a team of individuals through
  whom the ministry's tasks are fulfilled. It is not just an administrative
  designation but a fundamental difference in how they define church,
  ministry, and the pastor's relationship to it. A church led by a pastor-
  shepherd will typically be small, because regardless of how efficient an
  individual may be, they are still an individual, and hence the bulk of the
  ministry's responsibilities are under the oversight of a solo leader. However, a Christian education pastor *must* be a rancher. There are no solo
  Christian education leaders. The Christian educator is a pastor-rancher
  because if they are to effectively develop and direct a Sunday morning
  teaching venue, small groups, and midweek teaching and discipleship
  opportunities, not to mention other niche and/or age-related ministries,
  they require a team that serves and leads alongside them. The Christian
  educator is by nature a rancher.

While we have looked at the biblical basis for ministry and the distinctives
of what makes someone suited for a Christian education ministry, what pro-
fessionally identifies a Christian education pastor? Additionally, what makes
Christian education a Christian profession?[2]

First, a sense of *calling*—that a person has experienced or been led to a
time of reflection that recognizes God's special call on their life to serve in
a pastoral role.

Second, special *preparation* to fulfill the calling. The educational path of
a Christian educator is varied, but it might begin with a bachelor's degree,
followed by studying in a seminary, earning an MA in Christian education, a
master's in religious education, or even an MDiv with a Christian education
specialization. One may even continue onward to doctoral studies, with a
DMin, EdD, or PhD. Christian education is a professional pastoral role because

there is a specific pathway for preparation that extends from the local church through Christian higher education.

Third, career *placement* into a full-time pastoral role. A career in Christian education has a variety of options both in the local church, with all the ministry venues mentioned previously, and outside the local congregation, with Christian camps, educational resource production and publication, and even serving in Christian higher education. The ready availability of ministry opportunities is another way to demonstrate the viability of a Christian education ministry.

Fourth, and finally, *professional support* for pastors in Christian education continues to provide attention to their ministries. Without oversimplifying it, congregations provide salaries and compensation for those who will minister in Christian education. Likewise, there are resources such as conferences, seminars, journals, and books that are designed to update, encourage, and motivate the Christian educator, supporting their professional development as well as spiritual vitality. Professional development can take advantage of numerous resources and opportunities in the field of Christian education. Christian education *is* ministry; we just *do* ministry in a distinctive way!

Christian Education Is *More* than Teaching

Consider that in most congregations, when all the components of Christian education are taken into consideration, this ministry has the largest portion of the church's budget (after salaries and perhaps mortgage) and typically involves more volunteers than all the other ministries (serving in a wider variety of ministries), while utilizing more of the congregation's facilities than other ministries. Not to mention that those volunteering in the ministry of Christian education are usually among some of the most trained and equipped members of the congregation. Practicing Christian education requires a person called by God and supported by the church to fulfill this ministry. But make no mistake, Christian education is ministry!

Reflection Questions

1. How did this chapter change or challenge your understanding of ministry in general, or specifically Christian education ministry?

2. How resistant to or accepting of God's call are you? Did you first resist? Do you still have moments of concern and doubt about call? If so, what and why?

3. What concerns you most about entering ministry in the Christian education field?

4. How do you plan on continuing professional development in Christian education?

Suggestions for Further Reading

Browning, Robert L. *The Pastor as Religious Educator*. Birmingham, AL: Religious Education Press, 1998.

Griggs, Henry, and Weston Smith. *The Pastor at Work in Christian Education*. Philadelphia: Judson, 1930.

Munro, Harry C. *The Pastor and Religious Education*. Nashville: Abingdon, 1930.

Vanhoozer, Kevin J., and Owen Strachan. *The Pastor as Public Theologian: Reclaiming a Lost Vision*. Grand Rapids: Baker Academic, 2015.

Learning to Be a Christian

Can you learn to be a Christian? This is a crucial question for Christian educators. How we answer this question determines what we think we're supposed to do (and not do) as teachers, mentors, disciple makers, small group leaders, and so on. This *isn't* a trick question or a loaded question. Depending on how you define terms, interpret intentions, and emphasize words, the question could be read differently. Can you as a teacher, *alone*, apart from the Holy Spirit, teach someone to become a Christian? Is learning *just* knowledge, or is there more to it? Is it a change of mind, alone, or does it involve more? Likewise, is it learning to *be* a Christian, or to *become* a Christian? This chapter will introduce the idea of learning in the church, explaining how not all learning is alike and how learning requires different educational and pastoral approaches.

Learning through Concept Development

Second Timothy 3 mentions that Scripture can "make you wise" (v. 15) by providing information that can inform and form our thinking, moving us from being informed to thinking wisely. This is what educators call *cognitive learning*. We often use the metaphor of the head—that is, head knowledge. Scripture provides insight into this kind of learning. The preface to Proverbs explains that the purpose of learning is far beyond simply providing information but should result in concept development, building, connecting, and increasing in complexity as we study. Proverbs 1:1–7 reads:

The proverbs of Solomon, son of David, king of Israel:
To know wisdom and instruction,
    to understand words of insight,
to receive instruction in wise dealing,
    in righteousness, justice, and equity;
to give prudence to the simple,
    knowledge and discretion to the youth—
Let the wise hear and increase in learning,
    and the one who understands obtain guidance,
to understand a proverb and a saying,
    the words of the wise and their riddles.
The fear of the LORD is the beginning of knowledge;
    fools despise wisdom and instruction.

The author brings up everything from those who "despise wisdom" (v. 7), to those who think simply (v. 4), to those able to think with discernment (v. 4) and understanding (vv. 5, 6) and apply it to life (v. 5). This is all a portrait of the development of concepts, from knowing the content provided to thinking it through into a mind that exhibits wisdom. It is learning through concept development. The Bible itself exemplifies this, since as God's special verbal revelation, it calls us to cognitive learning. As Gerhard Bussmann writes, "God has appeared in history via events, appeared personally in Christ, and has also revealed his will via a written record, the Bible. . . . [Cognitive learning] is knowing God with the mind."[1]

Levels of "Knowing"

A third-grade children's church student might say, "I know John 3:16. 'For God so loved the world . . .'" Yes, they know it, in the sense they have memorized the words. However, if they are still at this level of cognition when they are adolescents or young adults, their knowledge may not serve to advance their faith. A seminary student might be able to say, "I know John 3:16 as it fits into the greater concept of 'love' in the writings of John." Both of these examples are cognitive learning, but they demonstrate the development of the concept. Benjamin Bloom formulated a six-tiered progression of knowledge to help us understand concept development—cognitive learning—from lower to higher orders of thinking.[2]

   1. *Knowledge*: like memorization, a rote knowledge of the subject
   2. *Comprehension*: the ability to translate, interpret, or extrapolate

3. *Application*: the ability to use the information in other situations
4. *Analysis*: the ability to discern elements and relationships and the organizational principle(s) behind an idea
5. *Synthesis*: combining the information with existing understanding; formulating a more abstract concept from the information
6. *Evaluation*: the ability to make judgments and to discern; wisdom

Bloom's taxonomy of cognitive learning demonstrates how learning is constructed, growing in complexity and interconnectedness until it reaches a comprehensive, consistent way of thinking. It allows educators to assess the student's level of thinking. This is based on a learning theory called *constructivism*. Constructivism basically emphasizes students' cognitive assembling of knowledge and understanding to ultimately make meaning. The learner is endeavoring to make sense of their world and construct that meaning. Cognitive theorists maintain that learning is the reorganization of perceptions. Knowledge is constructed when the learner recognizes relationships and makes connections between pieces of information and between bodies of knowledge, moving from isolated ideas to an interconnected concept.[3] Perhaps the most relevant theorists for constructivism are Jean Piaget and George Kelly, as well as Lev Vygotsky, who emphasized the role of society in the construction of meaning.

How does this impact practicing Christian education? Because faith has a cognitive dimension, learning about the faith is essential to becoming a Christian and continuing to grow in Christ. We need to know the story of Scripture. How can we expect people to think Christianly if they don't know the basics of our faith? As Christian educators, we need to help students learn to think in biblical and theological categories to facilitate biblical thinking. But what if this is overemphasized? What if this is the only kind of learning going on in a church? It can lead to one's faith being tied to legalism, a dehydrated orthodoxy, quasi-gnostic—brains on a stick. Learning to be a Christian would be reduced to having a head knowledge of faith with nothing else. Faith would be the facts and just the facts. This is why we must give attention to the other two ways in which we can learn.

Learning through Experiences

"Now when they heard this they were cut to the heart" (Acts 2:37). While learning may indeed be cognitive, it is also *affective*. Not effective, but affective, meaning it changes the heart—values, convictions, priorities, relationships, and commitments. Second Timothy 3 also says Scripture is "profitable for" a Christian life. We are not talking about learning by doing (that's next) but learning through life experiences. It is not just knowing Jesus with the mind, but "Whoever believes in the Son of God has the testimony in himself" (1 John 5:10). But how does "the heart" learn? It learns through experience.

Lawrence Richards describes the Mosaic idea of nurture as one replete with intentional experiences, all designed to immerse children into the faith experiences of their ancestors.[4] The learning in the faith community of both testaments took place through the calendar, festivals, feasts, and activities of remembrance. These celebrations of the covenant relationship with God in Old Testament feasts and festivals were a means of knowing God through his covenant. In the New Testament it happens through the Lord's Supper. The Bible presents a model of learning based on experiences, designed to shape the heart, such as experiencing God within the fellowship of the church, the Christian family, and the presence of the Holy Spirit, as well as on Christian holidays that are celebrations of the covenant.[5] Similarly, relationships provide a catalyst for affective learning through experience. Bussmann observes, "God has also chosen to make himself personally known to humanity. . . . Knowing God not only involves remembering his great acts in history, but experiencing the relationships he has desired for humanity."[6]

Levels of Affective Learning

As with cognitive learning, some have undertaken to describe the process or level of affective growth in the learner. David Krathwohl formulated a five-tiered taxonomy for explaining and evaluating learning in the affective domain. His model is as follows.[7]

1. *Receiving (attending)* occurs when someone is willing to listen, shows an awareness of another, and basically is willing to give someone or something attention. It's willingness to hear a new value.
2. *Responding* not only acknowledges a new idea but interacts with it by questioning, responding, and receiving a satisfactory response to it. The new value is now not so "new."
3. *Valuing* makes the transitional point of accepting the new idea. One accepts the value as one's own, making it a preference and making a commitment to it.
4. *Organization* happens when the newly affirmed and accepted value begins to influence one's life and one begins to restructure and reorganize one's values, commitments, and relationships.

5. *Characterization by a value or value complex* occurs when the value has taken such a firm presence in one's life that one exemplifies that value, or the value characterizes the person. What was once a value only to be listened to, one's life is now all about.

Krathwohl's taxonomy actually explains the process of conversion better than other taxonomies and theories of learning. We were once willing to listen to the gospel, entertain the message, and accept Christ for ourselves (valuing), and then he began to transform our lives until we became more and more Christlike (characterization).[8]

The learning theories that parallel or inform learning in the affective domain are described as *humanist* learning theories, which we'll describe in greater detail in chapter 11. Affective learning focuses on the individual and personal clarification of experiences and values, and learning theories that are more aligned with secular humanism emphasize this domain of learning. Affective learning is more value-driven, more prescriptive, rather than descriptive. Education usually has a low "core" and is heavy on electives because it is student centered.[9] For this reason teachers are described as facilitators rather than authority figures. Humanist learning theories are most associated with the ideas of psychologists Carl Rogers and Abraham Maslow, child educator John Hold, and adult educators Malcolm Knowles and Jack Mezirow, as well as Brazilian educator Paulo Freire.

How does this affect us practicing Christian education? Experiences, especially Christian ones, are crucial to forming faith. How many congregations sponsor cross-cultural mission trips to provide a unique ministry experience designed to challenge believers and facilitate growth? How many congregations emphasize the formation of community and building of relationships through small group ministries? The key to helping believers learn affectively through experience is to identify the desired values, attitudes, or characteristics and then provide the experiences that are most likely to elicit or stimulate these outcomes, even providing a role model or some information to help them process the experience and encourage the acceptance of change.

When one reflects on affective learning theory and strategies, the church's practical function and necessity become even more evident. The church models and provides an experience of a real, living faith. While experience may not be able to teach propositional truth, which is essentially cognitive, it does aid in the application and practical expression of belief. Learning through experience calls us as educators to become increasingly aware of our own life experience and the experiences of our students. Life experience teaches us, but often we are unaware of it, and hence as Christian educators we need to assist students in reflecting theologically on their life experience by raising probative and reflective questions.

One caution. When the affective domain is dominant in your approach to discipleship, it can result in a faith that is superficial, experiential, and rather self-centered. Faith lacks depth intellectually because of the focus on emotional engagement. As Paul critiques his Jewish countrymen, "I bear them witness that they have a zeal for God, but not according to knowledge" (Rom. 10:2).

Learning through Doing

However, while we can learn through the head and the heart, we now need to learn with our hands, metaphorically speaking. Learning can be done by doing something, through what we might call training. When you learned to tie your shoes, it was quite an accomplishment. You tried, but failed. Someone then showed you how to do it and asked you to try with their step-by-step instruction and feedback. Eventually, you were able to do it on your own. You became so proficient at tying your shoes that it's now automatic; you don't have to work at it, it just happens. In fact, slowing down to explain it to others can actually cause you to make a mistake! One can acquire a new ability or skill only by actually practicing it. Could you really learn to tie your shoes if someone came out with a lectern and PowerPoint slides about the history and philosophy of shoes, diagrams of shoes and laces, and videos of how one ties one's shoes—and if, upon listening and watching all this, you were then handed a pair of sneakers and told to tie them? No! To really master a skill you have to repeatedly practice it with assistance and feedback until you no longer need either. This is learning by doing.

In the Old Testament, the skills needed to produce the tabernacle were lacking, and the need was so urgent that God gifted individuals with the skills to do what needed to be done without any prior training (Exod. 35:30–35). Conversely, Jesus's ministry with the Twelve gives insight into the process of training others. As one reads Mark's Gospel, early on Jesus is doing everything, and the disciples are spectators (1:14–3:12). The disciples begin to assist Jesus in what he is doing (3:13–6:6). Then, once they know what to do, the disciples begin doing the ministry while Jesus supervises them (6:7–13, 30). At the close of the Gospel, the disciples are commissioned to do the ministry as Jesus departs—the Great Commission (16:15–16, 20). Jesus didn't just lecture them or let them observe his ministry; he trained them to do ministry by letting them do it with him. They were learning by doing.

Levels of Skill Learning

Perhaps one of the greatest challenges of discussing learning by doing is the labeling of the learning domain itself. Some call it *behavioral*, others *psycho-motor*, others *active* or *skill*. Likewise, because "doing" is very general yet sometimes specific to a certain set of skills, each requiring varying levels of expertise, numerous "taxonomies" for this kind of learning have developed. Unlike scholars of the cognitive and affective, those who study learning by doing have not widely accepted any one taxonomy. Figure 7.1 summarizes an analysis of these taxonomies.

Figure 7.1
Taxonomies of Learning

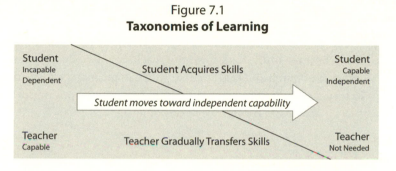

Just like when you learned to tie your shoes, the teacher works with the student, who becomes more capable and less reliant on the teacher until the student is capable of performing the task on their own. The taxonomies often denote the step-by-step development of the student's capabilities, usually in five tiers, but label them distinctively depending on the skill on which the taxonomy is based. One learning theory that lends itself well to learning by practicing is that of Russian theorist Lev Vygotsky. He theorized learning in "zones": the zone of potential development, the zone of actual development, and finally the zone of proximal development. The student has a potential for development, but that is usually more than their actual development—that is, what the student is able to do at present is not their full potential. The distance between these two zones is the area of proximal development, which is the area needed to close the gap, wherein the teacher provides insight, guidance, practice, and feedback until the student meets their full potential and is able to accomplish the task themselves. While Vygotsky used his zones to describe even cognitive development, the acquiring of skills obviously is addressed in his writing.[10] Often the behavioral theories of learning are relevant to the psychomotor or behavior domain of learning, beginning with the theories of Ivan Pavlov and B. F. Skinner. These theories focus on the motivation of the student toward a desired behavior or action through the introduction of rewards and punishments for performance designed to reinforce learning.[11]

What does this have to do with practicing Christian education? Not everything about the Christian faith can be taught in a classroom or experienced in a prayer meeting. Part of our education ministry has to be about training believers in the skills necessary for their faith and for active participation in ministry. Learning to do something new requires them to actively participate, but only with guidance and feedback from a capable teacher, to develop their own abilities and reach their potential, cultivating good performance while correcting underperformance.

As with the other learning domains, a danger exists in emphasizing this kind of learning over the others. Focusing exclusively on learning through doing can lead to a very outward-focused, works-oriented Christian faith. Education can become utilitarian, meaning teaching only what is needed to do the work of the church and nothing else, and can ultimately contribute to burnout in terms of commitment to perpetual service without opportunity for cognitive or affective learning. We need balance.

Your Congregation Is a Learning Organization

While there is more to faith than learning, the teaching ministry of the church can indeed advance, nurture, and equip the believer to grow in faith. Your congregation is a learning organization. Believers develop a Christian worldview—God's perspective on life—by forming a Christian intellect and learning through concept development. Believers develop values, passion, convictions, and character as they engage in Christian experiences and relationships, growing affectively by learning through experiences. They also grow in their abilities, the practices of the Christian faith, and their personal ministries when they are guided and trained by a more mature teacher, developing proficient practices for growth and service as they learn through doing. The church must embrace and find balance in all three ways we learn, or else learning in the church will result in an overemphasis and imbalance in our faith. Practicing Christian education involves utilizing all three approaches, emphasizing the one most relevant for a specific program, but not to the exclusion of the other two.

Reflection Questions

1. How would you teach someone about an apple if they had never even seen one (cognitive learning)? Be creative. How might this apply to teaching the Bible's content?
2. How would you teach someone to ride a bike (skill learning)? Be creative. How might this apply to teaching for service?
3. How would you teach someone to be kind (affective learning)? Be creative. How might this apply to teaching for piety and character formation?
4. How might a Sunday school class or small group embrace all three types of learning? What would this require them to.do differently?
5. How might a teacher/sponsor/leader development program embrace all three types of learning? Why not just learning through doing?
6. Review the ministry programs in your home or current congregation. What kind of learning do they promote? Are these in balance, or is there an imbalance?

Suggestions for Further Reading

Moreno, Roxeno. *Educational Psychology.* Hoboken, NJ: Wiley, 2010.

Slavin, Robert E. *Educational Psychology: Theory and Practice.* Boston: Allyn and Bacon, 2000.

Yount, William. *Created to Learn.* 2nd ed. Nashville: B&H, 2012.

Scripture as Formation

The Bible is central to practicing Christian education. It is God's specific revelation that reveals God's story of salvation. We believe that the truths in Scripture provide a means to help ascertain matters of salvation as they relate to Christian faith and practice. However, even though Christians assert the authority of the Bible, in recent years the use of the Bible has declined in the church and in its formative practices such as worship and discipleship. Why?

Many Christians have reduced the Bible's primary role to a means to prove Christian doctrine, a source for debates and theological dialogues. Another reason is that the preferred approach to the Bible that has shaped much of biblical scholarship has focused on historical contexts. In other words, the primary focus of interpretation has been on "what the text meant," since Scriptures are written in a particular historical context. This approach illustrates that the Bible functions to clarify the theological *information* about the Christian faith. The primary focus of this type of interpretation is on studying the Bible as a means of gathering appropriate information. This is not completely bad, but it limits the role of Scripture. However, fortunately for practicing Christian education, more current interpretations of Scripture have more to do with the formative role. This approach to interpretation focuses on "what the text means" to the reader. As we read the Bible, we are experiencing God through our reading. This formative approach to interpretation is much closer to the early church's view of Scripture as transformative and formative. The early church recognized that Scripture was given to the church to transform and form persons into Christlikeness.[1] This means that the Scriptures themselves and their proper use in the church are an indispensable element for practicing Christian education.

Practicing Christian Education with Scripture

The formative role of Scripture affirms that just as the Holy Spirit was active in inspiring the authors of the Bible (2 Tim. 3:16; 2 Pet. 1:21), the Spirit illuminates the person who reads and interprets the text (1 Cor. 2:14; John 14:26; 16:13). Some Bible scholars refer to this as *double inspiration* to describe the Spirit's special activity in the writing of Scripture and the Spirit's general activity in guiding the reader of Scripture. So when we read the Bible, the Holy Spirit is active to enlighten us to discern the will of God through a particular text of Scripture. This cooperative process between the reader and the Spirit helps us discover potential meaning about God and God's ongoing work of salvation. Therefore, given that the Bible functions in *formative ways*, practicing Christian education calls us to consistently read and engage the Scriptures. And when we do, we move from viewing the Bible primarily as a means of information to experiencing the formative power of Scripture that transforms our lives.

Where does formative reading take place? While it can be done alone, as solo reading, it is best done in community. The Bible is not meant to be read in isolation but in the context of Christian community. Why? In some cases, our Western context fosters an individualistic view of faith isolated from the Christian community. But it is within Christian community that Scripture is to be read, interpreted, and applied to our lives. The goal is that Scripture will speak to that community, in our context, in a meaningful and redemptive way.

Formative Bible Practices in Practicing Christian Education

The shift from viewing Scripture as *information* to *formation* can be a difficult transition. One of the primary roles of Christian educators is to help believers understand the difference between these two approaches. It's a challenge because many of us have it ingrained in us to approach Scripture reading as informational, to uncover certain biblical ideas or truths, a purely cognitive pursuit. We have been taught to read Scripture so as to master the text instead of having the text master us, or viewing Scripture as a means of formation. Christian educators need to help believers reorient how they approach and encounter Scripture. They must also help believers develop formative practices in their faith journeys and within the life of the church community. The goal is that through reading and interpreting Scripture, we are being formed and transformed into faithful disciples of Jesus Christ.

What does this mean for practicing Christian education? It means that any of us, regardless of our level of biblical expertise, can read the Bible and encounter God. In this regard, formational reading includes opening ourselves to the text to allow the Bible to intrude into our life, to allow ourselves to be addressed and encountered by it. Instead of mastering the text through study, formational reading invites the text to master and form us. We come to the text open to hear, to receive, to respond to, and to serve the Word. Sandra Schneiders asserts that biblical spirituality indicates a transformative process for the individual and communal engagement with the biblical text. The nonspecialist can approach the text not merely as a historical record or even as a literary medium but as the Word of God.[2] When we read the Bible as formation, we find new excitement and energy in a text that we perhaps once viewed as boring and irrelevant.

Practicing Christian education means we have to foster a variety of practices so that Scripture forms and transforms faithful disciples, but two major areas in which Scripture functions formatively are explored in this chapter: Bible reading and Bible study (*lectio divina* and inductive Bible study), and worship (preaching and Scripture reading).

Sacred Reading (Lectio Divina)

Spiritual reading is a meditative approach to the written Word. It requires unhurried time and an open heart. The purpose of sacred reading is for God to work on us, and for us to be open to his formative work in our lives. For this to take place requires both the practice of attentive listening and a willingness to respond to what we hear. The Scriptures were written for the purpose of presenting us with God's Word, and the purpose of spiritual reading is to allow ourselves to be addressed by God's Word. They are completely consonant and interconnected.

One ancient practice that has reemerged as a formative process for engaging Scripture is *lectio divina* (sacred reading). The origin of the practice can be traced back to the desert fathers and mothers, whose spirituality consisted primarily of prayerful rumination on biblical texts.[3] This practice was later developed by the Benedictine monasteries, ordered around the Rule of Saint Benedict (ca. 540). With a rediscovery of ancient spiritual practices, many Christians today are practicing this aspect of formational reading as a means to make Bible reading exciting and engaging once again.

Lectio divina is a process of scriptural encounter that includes a series of prayer dynamics that move the reader to a deep level of engagement with the chosen text and with the Spirit, who enlivens the text.[4] The process includes the following movements:

1. *Silencio* (silence): *Lectio divina* begins by approaching the passage in open, receptive listening, reading silently. The reader takes time for silent prayer.

2. *Lectio* (reading): The next movement is to read the text aloud, slowly and deliberately, to evoke imagination. Hearing the text reminds the hearer of the spoken Word of God. The text can be read two or three times by both men and women to hear different aspects of the text.

3. *Meditatio* (meditation): Following the reading of the Scripture is a time of silent meditation. To meditate is to think about or mentally chew on what has been read for a period of time. In the past, this process often included the commitment of the text to memory. By internalizing the text in its verbal form, one passes on to a rumination or meditation on its meaning.

4. *Oratio* (prayer): Because the text is engaged in experiential terms, the meditation gives rise to a prayerful response to God, who speaks in and through the text.

5. *Contemplatio* (contemplation): The next movement is contemplation. It is here that the participant is in union with God through the Spirit. In contemplation, the person stops and rests silently before God, receiving whatever the Spirit gives.

6. *Compassio* (compassion): This final movement of sacred reading is acted out through acts of love toward others. Whatever insight, feeling, or commitment emerges from time with Scripture is to be shared as grace with others.

Lectio divina is a practice that can be experienced regularly to transform a person into the likeness of Christ encountered in Scripture. Christian educators can help us develop this spiritual practice either individually or corporately. In either case, *lectio divina* provides a direct and subjective encounter with Scripture that forms and transforms our lives.

Scripture in Bible Studies and Small Groups

Bible studies or small groups provide a context for deepening relationships and connectedness. In fact, Christian education is usually done in small groups and Bible studies. Humans are created in the image and likeness of God (*imago Dei*) as relational beings who value close relationship with others. Humans reflect the very nature of the Triune God, as relational beings in need of acceptance, love, and care. John Wesley, the founder of the Methodist movement, believed that there could be no personal holiness without social holiness.[5] He was referring to *koinonia*, "fellowship." Christian formation takes place best in social contexts.

Our Christian life is not a solitary journey but a pilgrimage made in the company of other believers. Although small groups have a wide range of purposes and approaches, one of the primary resources for shaping the life of the church emerges from Bible study in small groups.[6] A biblical spirituality represents a transformative process of personal and communal engagement with the biblical text. For people with a limited knowledge of the Bible, reading and studying the Bible in the context of an intimate group gives opportunities for learning and Christian growth. People who will not read the Bible on their own may read it in the context of a small group. Also, studying the Bible in a small group helps people broaden and deepen their understanding of a given passage, while guarding against misleading individual interpretations of Scripture. Scripture should always be interpreted and understood in the context of community to help prevent misinterpretation. Studying the Bible in a group also helps people make meaning of their faith by verbalizing what the Bible means and how it applies to a life of faith. On their own, people easily ignore the relationship of biblical truth to their own lives. In a group setting, people talk about Scripture together, which helps them apply what they are learning to their lives.[7]

Christian educators can give focus to studying the Bible in groups as a central aspect of Christian discipleship. We gather to study Scripture regularly with a wide range of methods and approaches. One approach to Bible study is a *deductive approach*. A deductive approach tends to be subjective and prejudicial. In this approach, the reader comes to the Bible with conclusions, then goes to the text to find proof for those ideas. The result is that the reader dictates to Scripture rather than listening to the Scripture.[8]

On the other hand, an *inductive approach* to Bible study strives to interpret the Bible honestly, examining the particulars of Scripture before making conclusions. The inductive approach to Bible study produces people who hear and listen to the text. An inductive approach allows the reader to interpret the Bible through observation and reflection, drawing out ideas and truths in Scripture. A person learns by examining the objects of the study themselves and drawing one's own conclusions about these materials from that direct encounter with them.[9] This approach allows the interpreter to discover the

Word of God and internalize their discoveries, resulting in formation and transformation.

Practicing Christian education provides opportunities for faithful disciples to gather in small groups and Bible studies to struggle over how to interpret and apply Scripture today. Also, Christian educators recognize that the Holy Spirit is active in the community to form and shape faithful disciples. Bible studies can incite readers to discern the deep meaning of the text and its implications for daily life. The practice of inductive Bible study, both personally and corporately, is a means of spiritual growth.

Scripture in Worship

Worship is often viewed separate from the church's Christian education ministry; but ironically, when it is children's church or teen worship, suddenly it's part of practicing Christian education. But don't we learn something from worship? We can encounter the transformative reading of Scripture in worship through a variety of practices. First, we engage Scripture through the preaching of the Word. In the early church, preaching preceded the writing of the New Testament texts. The eyewitnesses of the Christ event testified to what they had seen and heard. Preaching touched and transformed the early Christians' lives. In the same way today, when the Bible is preached, our lives are changed and transformed through the work of the Holy Spirit. The idea of the Word emphasizes the proclamation of Scripture as the spoken Word of God that bears witness to the incarnate Word in Jesus Christ. But it is not simply that it bears witness. The spoken Word becomes the living and active Word of God so that God speaks anew through the spoken Word of Scripture. In this sense, the spoken Word becomes a means for spiritual growth; it is formative. The preacher speaks *for* God, *from* the Scriptures, *by* the authority of the church, *to* the people. God speaks through the proclamation of the Word, through the inspiration of Scripture, to provide healing and reconciliation.[10] The preacher interprets Scripture for the community, placing it within the larger narrative of the biblical witness, and helps believers make meaning for life. Scriptural preaching allows believers to hear and discover their role in the broader narrative of God's redemptive work in the world.

In our Protestant faith tradition, preaching is central to liturgy. Many Protestant congregations follow the lectionary and the Christian calendar. The lectionary is a three-year cycle that moves through the story of Scripture. The Christian calendar includes the primary Christian festivals, beginning with Advent and ending with Christ the King Sunday. Sacred days include Epiphany, Pentecost, Ash Wednesday, Lent, and Holy Week. The role of Christian educators is to ensure that the congregation's worship includes aspects of the Christian calendar.

Second, Scripture is encountered through the worship service. It is the Bible, read and preached and received, that calls the Christian community together to worship. When we are gathered around Scripture, it becomes the heart of Christian worship. Without Christian worship, there would be no Bible. In a very real sense, the Bible is the product of the early church's common prayer. Stories of the life and ministry of Jesus and the early apostles were circulated among the earliest Christian communities and read in common worship so they could hear and respond.[11] In the same way, the interrelationship between worship and the Scriptures is evident today as Scripture is preached, read, and experienced in worship. It is through worship, as the community of faith gathers, that Scripture comes to life.

Congregations that follow the Christian calendar and lectionary readings provide us with an opportunity to participate in the story of God. The reading of Scripture is an interpretative act that provides an opportunity for us to encounter God. It is ironic that some Christians who view Scripture as primary and authoritative for faith and practice do not practice regular reading of Scripture in worship. In order for Scripture to be formative in the life of the church, it must be read, experienced, and interpreted in the worshiping community. Also, responsive readings, hymns, and choral music (assuming they have a biblical basis) provide an avenue for worshipers to interact with the Scripture.

Conclusion

For many Christians, the Bible has become irrelevant, boring, and disconnected from their faith. This may be caused by the church's inability to educate and model for believers that Scripture is less about information and more about formation and transformation. Christians who view Scripture in formative ways can experience and encounter Scripture in new and fresh ways. Since Christian education has a formative view of Scripture, Christian educators should develop practices in Bible reading, Bible study, preaching, and worship that are formative in nature. When this occurs, the church becomes the primary context within which Scripture functions in formative ways. Practicing Christian education aims to educate believers so that they develop a formative view of Scripture that shapes the way we think about God and ourselves, and how Christians respond to one another and the world around them. The Bible speaks as sacred Scripture by calling us to respond in faithful ways in light of biblical provocations to faithful living. The formative role of Scripture necessitates an obedient response to its call for holy living. Christian educators who view Scripture in formative ways provide Christians with opportunities to encounter the Bible in fresh and new ways that form and transform them into faithful disciples.

Reflection Questions

1. In what ways is reading Scripture as formation different from reading Scripture as information? How do you make the shift to reading Scripture as formation?
2. In what ways can you balance individual and communal reading and studying of Scripture?
3. What is *lectio divina*? How can you apply this practice to your spiritual growth?
4. What is the difference between inductive and deductive Bible study?
5. In what ways can you include Scripture in worship?

Suggestions for Further Reading

Adam, A. K. M. *Faithful Interpretation: Reading the Bible in a Postmodern World.* Minneapolis: Fortress, 2006.

Fowl, Stephen E., and L. Gregory Jones. *Reading in Communion: Scripture and Ethics in Christian Life.* Grand Rapids: Eerdmans, 1991.

Hestenes, Roberta. *Using the Bible in Groups.* Philadelphia: Westminster, 1983.

Mulholland, M. Robert. *Shaped by the Word: The Power of Scripture in Spiritual Formation.* Nashville: Upper Room Books, 2000.

Thompson, Marjorie J. *Soul Feast: An Invitation to the Christian Spiritual Life.* Louisville: Westminster John Knox, 1995.

Congregational Education and Formation

The most formative aspects of our faith take place within the context of local congregations. As Christians, we are shaped and formed through the practices, activities, and events of the local church. Practicing Christian education involves social gatherings, Bible studies, worship, and service, which all play an important role in forming our faith. Some have said that it takes a village to raise a child; in the same way, it takes a congregation to form a Christian. In this respect, the practices and activities of a local congregation are critical in faith formation. So why do some congregations do a better job of faith formation than other congregations? What are the specific practices and activities in these congregations that shape faith? These questions become critical in understanding what it really means to do Christian education comprehensively in local congregations, which, by God's grace, form and shape people's faith.

What is *congregational formation*? Congregational formation is primarily concerned with how, through its practices, the community of faith forms and transforms Christians. Congregations serve a distinct mission, providing a sacred place where God's Spirit promises to dwell among believers. Congregational formation exists to "build up," to construct communities of faith that serve God and love neighbors, for the sake of transforming the world. Congregational formation describes the corporate educational effort that nurtures and forms the faith and the witness of community members.[1]

Corporate Memory

Each local congregation possesses a unique personality or history that shapes what its members believe and how they practice their faith. Congregations exist in diverse groups of faith traditions and denominations, each reflecting a particular aspect of the vision and mission of the church. For example, a congregation shapes its identity when it focuses more on social justice and compassionate ministries. Or a congregation shapes the ethos and identity of a local church when it gives more attention to the sacramental practices.

In the same way that families have a memory of the events and activities of their past, so do congregations. Congregations have a *corporate memory*. This corporate memory provides the primary avenue to pass beliefs on to the next generation. Practicing Christian education in local churches requires us to pass on the beliefs, practices, and values to other believers, especially the next generation. This includes the biblical and theological traditions of that particular faith community. Who we are and what we believe influences how the congregation shapes and forms faith. In essence, we are a product of our local congregation or tribe. Congregational memory includes the recognition of our place in the faith tradition and how that tradition will be carried on to the next generation.

Charles Foster expresses concern that congregations continue to lose corporate memory, especially with the loss of connectedness across generations and the diminishing loyalty to faith communities.[2] Many congregations lose their memory due to the increasing number of new people attending church. Recognizing, preserving, and developing memory remains one of the primary purposes and tasks of congregational formation.

The Christian educator is to provide intentional practices that ensure the corporate memory of a congregation, which includes its beliefs, values, and practices, is passed on to the next generation. This becomes especially important given that many new attenders do not have an understanding of the Bible, theology, or Christian practices. In other words, they do not have a sense of memory about the faith tradition. Therefore, Christian education needs to intentionally ensure that new believers are taught about the faith tradition. This is best done through modeling Christian practices that are important in teaching the faith story.

Community as Formation

Forming faith in congregations includes the development of biblical community. An important biblical passage regarding community is Acts 2:42: "And they devoted themselves to the apostles' teaching and the fellowship, to the breaking of bread and the prayers." Christians often view this passage as the beginning of the church because it represents the first example in Scripture after Pentecost of believers gathering together for worship and fellowship. The passage focuses on four qualities of this new church: the apostles' teachings, fellowship, breaking of bread, and prayers. These four qualities are reflected in the formation of many congregations.

The passage provides two distinct pairs that are linked together. The first pair is "the apostles' teachings" and "fellowship," or *koinonia*. The *apostles' teachings* refers to the testimony or witness of the Twelve about Jesus's ministry and resurrection. *Fellowship* was common in the Greco-Roman world and referred to the relation or bond between persons. This passage focuses on the bond among all the groups of believers.

The second pair is "the breaking of bread" and "prayers," and has similar connections. The *breaking of bread* doesn't refer to taking Communion together, as some interpreters have suggested; rather, it focuses on believers sharing a meal together at someone's home. It is representative of how many congregations gather together around a meal or potluck. *The prayers* refers to times of prayer in the temple for worship and times of prayer among believers. Both of these pairs provide a connection between worshipful activities and the social bond between believers as they gather in homes for prayer and a meal.[3] Luke further describes the communal life of the ancient church in Acts 2:44–45, observing that everyone had everything in common and shared their resources. They gave to anyone in need. This communal approach to living was a characteristic of the early Christians.

The ancient church example in Acts provides a basis for Christian community or *koinonia*. *Koinonia* means "communion," "participation," or "joint participation." In the New Testament, the word means that the collective well-being of the community supersedes the self-interest of the individual members. In other words, everyone is to work and produce for the sake of the community. This has two primary implications for practicing Christian education today. First, *koinonia* means that Christians are to gather together with other Christians for times of prayer, worship, fellowship, and to share a meal. Second, it refers to social equality. The early Christians understood that fellowship included the acceptance of all people regardless of their socioeconomic, ethnic, religious, gender, or cultural context. Their identity in Jesus Christ took precedence over social systems and classes of people. They shared their resources and viewed everyone as equal.

Community or *koinonia* has become more difficult in societies influenced by a Western individualistic mind-set. Many Christians maintain a privatized faith and believe they have no responsibility to other people or to a local congregation. Faith is often divorced from relationships with others. But as John Wesley believed, referring to the importance of social relationships within the context of community, there is no holiness without social holiness.[4] This includes the sharing of spiritual lives together in small groups as places of spiritual accountability.

Christian educators have an opportunity to speak to these challenges by creating a sense of community. Authentic community breaks through the fragmentation and individualism and provides a place for acceptance. Communities share a "common heritage" originating in God's love and grace, which binds all ages and diverse groups together. We need to practice Christian education in such a way as to preserve and advance the qualities of a distinctively formative Christian community.

Intergenerational Ministries

Practicing Christian education is obviously a generational ministry, involving children, adolescents, and adults of all ages, but often it is not *inter*generational. Many congregations have moved away from the segmentation of age groups to embrace intergenerational ministries. One example of this is the recent development of *Sticky Faith* by Karen Powell and Chap Clark.[5] Their thesis is that intergenerational ministry isn't something that congregations do; it is something they become. Christian educators and congregations need to value intergenerational relationships. In order for this to take place, there needs to be a shift away from an individualistic mind-set to develop a mind-set that includes assimilating children and youth into the church today. This shift does not mean moving away from age-level-specific ministries, but it means supplementing them with intentional intergenerational practices and activities.

For example, many youth ministers began to acknowledge that their ministries seemed isolated from the life of families and the general church, creating one-eared Mickey Mouse ministries that isolated youth from intergenerational influence.[6] So they have begun to develop activities and practices that include youth within the overall life of the congregation. These intergenerational forms of Christian education include the whole family.

The shift to intergenerational ministries has also included a focus on family ministry. One example of this is intergenerational forms of worship that include all age groups. Through worship, the stories, rituals, and symbols provide a means to remember the faith story and to "tell" the faith story to others. Congregation formation as family ministry includes providing education about the sacraments of baptism and the Eucharist as central aspects of the worshiping community. These sacraments foster faith formation in individuals and the family.

Another important aspect of intergenerational ministries is acts of compassion and service. All age groups can be engaged in mission projects and acts of justice. These can be some of the most formative events in a person's faith formation. When people have an opportunity to practice their faith with others, it can be very formative. Also, when faith is practiced within the context of the church, specific habits, beliefs, and behaviors are developed.

The benefit of intergenerational ministries is that they allow each generation the opportunity to learn from the others. An intergenerational ministry fosters activities for all age groups, providing opportunities for intergenerational formation. Children and youth can be nurtured and modeled by adults, while adults can listen to and learn from the younger generation. Congregational formation includes all ages in worshiping, learning, and serving together. This may be a challenge for congregations that have age-level ministries, but faithful discipleship includes finding creative avenues to integrate all generations.[7] Practicing Christian education in the contemporary congregation requires us not just to embrace believers of all ages—though we can never wholly abandon age-related ministries—but also to foster intergenerational opportunities for learning and relationships to facilitate formative Christian communities.

Catechesis

Catechesis describes the way Christians are made. It means all the intentional learning within a community of Christian faith and life. Historically, the mark of a Christian is our baptism. We spend the rest of our lives involved in a process of becoming more Christian. That lifelong process is one of catechesis. John Westerhoff describes catechesis as essentially a pastoral activity intended to transmit the church's tradition and to enable faith to become living, conscious, and active in the life of maturing persons and a maturing community.[8] It is concerned not only with conversion and nurture, commitment and behavior, but also with aiding the community to become more Christian. It is about passing on living tradition in the form of a story and vision for all those who share in the life and mission of the Christian faith community. Westerhoff affirms that "catechesis is the deliberate (intentional), systematic (related) and sustained (life-long) processes within the community of Christian faith and life which establish, build up, equip, and enable it to be

Christ's body or presence in the world to the end that all people are restored to unity with God and each other."[9] Catechesis is at the heart of practicing Christian education.

Westerhoff's view of catechesis includes three aspects: *formation, education*, and *instruction*.[10]

- *Formation* implies intentional, relational, and experiential activities within the life of the congregation. Examples include mission trips, service projects, and service learning.
- *Education* implies "reshaping" and refers to critical, reflective activities related to these communal experiences.
- *Instruction* implies "building" and refers to knowledge and skills useful to communal life that are transmitted, acquired, and understood through a teaching process.

These three distinct aspects are interrelated processes in catechesis. *Formation* is how the body of Christ is formed through intentional practices. *Christian education* is the process of reflecting on these practices; and *instruction* or *teaching* is the processes of building knowledge so the congregational corporate memory can be communicated. The goal of catechesis is to help Christians both individually and corporately grow in their relationship with God and in their relationship with other believers. The result is that as people grow spiritually, they will be engaged in acts of justice, mercy, and compassion.

Worship and Catechesis as Formation

Catechesis begins in worship. Worship remains central to congregational formation. In worship, people gather to give praise and thanksgiving to God. Many Christian educators believe that worship anchors formation and that all efforts of forming and discipling Christians should take place in worship.[11] Debra Dean Murphy believes that Christians are formed and transformed through worship, praise, and doxology. She argues that worship and Christian education often appear as two separate enterprises because Christian education has been influenced by modern models of education that divide worship and Christian education. Murphy's primary thesis calls for a catechesis that provides a richer theological heritage that unites Christian education and worship with discipleship and doxology. For Murphy, catechesis more fully captures the goal of Christian education as formation and transformation. Any formalized teaching about creed or doctrine must concede the primacy of worship for shaping people to be able to receive and understand such doctrinal instruction.[12]

A deep unity exists between Christian formation and worship, between discipleship and doxology. Catechesis is a journey of transformation that culminates in the praise and adoration of God. Catechesis begins and ends with liturgy, ultimately giving praise and worship to God. Thus worship confers and nurtures Christian identity. Therefore, corporate worship through preaching, prayer, and the sacraments provides a more robust form of congregational formation.

An important part of congregational formation through worship is the significant events within the worshiping community. Charles Foster identifies four events that form congregations and nurture faith: *paradigmatic events, seasonal events, occasional events*, and *unexpected events*.[13]

First, *paradigmatic events* establish a pattern for Christian life and community that have their origin in ancient traditions and rituals. These can include such events as caring for the poor and ministry to widows or widowers.

Second, *seasonal events* are rhythmic patterns of congregational formation that include following the Christian calendar. The ritual processes that structure these events carry the congregation through the liturgical seasons from Advent through Christmas, Epiphany, Lent, Easter, and Pentecost, and through saints' days. Observing seasons helps Christians "relive" Jesus's birth, ministry, death, resurrection, and ongoing ministry through the church. As we participate in the liturgical life of the church, we participate in the events of God's story of salvation.

There is a renewed interest in following the Christian calendar and lectionary readings in worship. The lectionary describes a list of Bible passages for reading, studying, or preaching in services of worship that cover the majority of Scripture in a three-year pattern. The lectionary readings usually include passages from the Old Testament, Psalms, Gospels, and Epistles. Following the lectionary provides an educational curriculum to tell the complete story of Scripture. In worshiping contexts, the lectionary is used to guide Scripture reading in worship and preaching. Congregational reading of Scripture provides an interpretive act that brings Scripture to the center of the worshiping community. The story of Scripture is also taught and experienced through preaching through the lectionary. The benefit of including the lectionary as a curriculum in worship is the retelling of the Christian story, which allows people to participate in the story each year.

Third, *occasional events* intensify community identity and mission by providing community meaning and life. These events include weddings, funerals, baptisms, anniversaries, mission trips, homecomings, and church building dedications.[14] For example, a community's identity is heightened when a young couple brings a child to be dedicated or baptized. Homecoming ceremonies provide a time of retelling the heritage of a congregation. Through these significant church events, faith formation takes place in the context of congregational practice.

Fourth, *unexpected events* include events that interrupt the rhythmic patterns and structures that give order to the worshiping community. These unexpected events bring joy and sorrow, blessing and suffering. They come in various forms, such as a tragic loss of life, the loss of employment, or a birth of a child with a disease. These unexpected events of life interrupt the normal flow of congregational life and worship,[15] and provide new meaning and understanding as the community responds to these situations.

Each of these movements or events forms and shapes lives as the community of faith worships and lives life together. Worship is formative and transformative as people engage in praise and adoration of God, as they hear the Scripture read and preached, and as they participate in the telling of the gospel story each week. All of this is crucial if practicing Christian education is going to foster congregational formation.

Word/Preaching and Table/Communion as Formation

Historically, as the church gathers for worship, it gathers around the proclamation of the Word through preaching and the Table for Communion. The combination of Word and Table provides important aspects of congregational formation. Many evangelical congregations identify more with the proclamation or preaching of the gospel than with regular participation in Communion. The reason for this is the influence of the Protestant Reformation, which emphasized a high view of Scripture and the proclamation of the gospel. In most evangelical congregations, preaching is central to the worshiping community. The proclamation of the gospel is a powerful means of forming and fostering faith among believers.

Regular participation in the Eucharist or Table doesn't replace the role of the Word in worship; rather, Eucharist provides balance in worship. The Table expands our understanding of and discourse about God's grace by including a living sign of the same gospel, now in tangible and visible form.[16]

With an increased interest in ancient and historical practices of the church, particularly as they relate to worship, many evangelical congregations are rediscovering the formative power of the Eucharist. One reason for this movement is the influence of postmodern forms of worship that place a great emphasis on experience, community, and mystery. Postmodern worship critiques modern approaches to worship that focus primarily on more cognitive and transmissive forms of worship. There is a greater emphasis and focus on the experiential aspects of Communion as a means to encounter the living God.

The role of the Christian educator is to help believers view the formative power of both proclamation and Communion. Most evangelical churches struggle with practicing Communion frequently, even weekly, because they reflect more of a "low" view of liturgy. However, as mentioned above, with a renewed interest in ancient practices, the Christian educator can help educate and equip congregations to understand the value of the formative role of Communion. This also reminds us that practicing Christian education involves more than teaching content; it also involves embracing and participating in the ancient practices of the church.

Baptism

Historically, baptism marked the entrance into the faith community. Someone believed and was baptized. Most evangelical congregations hold to two biblical sacraments: Communion and baptism. Communion is discussed above, and baptism in the modern evangelical tradition includes both infant and adult baptism.

Some faith traditions practice infant baptism as the beginning of the faith formation of a child. An infant is baptized and becomes a member of the faith community. In essence, their baptism makes them Christian. As a member of the faith community, the infant is nurtured and educated through the faith community. When the child reaches age twelve or thirteen, they will go through a confirmation class. The confirmation class includes instruction about the beliefs and practices of the faith tradition and provides an opportunity for the child to either affirm or reject their baptism.[17]

Some Christian faith traditions practice adult baptism. Adults who were *not* baptized as an infant are baptized for the first time. If a person *was* baptized as an infant, they can reaffirm their baptism as an adult. Adult baptism is more than a testimony of a person's faith; it is the dying to sin and being resurrected in Christ. Through baptism, adults receive grace from God that provides death to sin and resurrection in Jesus Christ. It is through baptism that the adult is empowered by the Holy Spirit to live a life of Christlikeness (Acts 2:38, 41; 8:12, 34–39; 22:16; Rom. 6:1–4; Gal. 3:26–27; Col. 2:11–12; 1 Pet. 3:21).[18]

Baptism, both infant and adult, is an important sacrament in which grace is received and the recipient becomes a member of the faith community.

Baptism is formative for the person and the faith community. When someone is baptized, it reminds all Christians of their baptism and provides an opportunity for them to reaffirm their baptism. Practicing Christian education, whether it is in a congregation that practices infant or adult baptism, requires the Christian educator to prepare individuals for baptism, facilitate the practice of baptism, and provide nurture and instruction following baptism.

Conclusion

We, the authors, are deeply appreciative of the local church's impact on our faith formation. It was through the strong sense of *koinonia* that we developed deep relationships that shaped our lives. The preaching, teaching, and worship provided challenge and renewal in our lives, and through weekly participation in Communion we received healing and renewal to live out God's mission in the world. More so, it was the preachers, the teachers, those who led and participated with us in worship, the examples and relationships that have shaped and mentored us in the Christian life. We are grateful that pastors and leaders were intentional about the practices that were incorporated in congregational formation. As you finish this chapter, we hope you will reflect on the ways in which your local congregation has shaped and formed your faith, and that you recognize the significant role it has in your life. As you do Christian education in your own ministry, do not forget this lesson.

The Christian educator's role is to value the importance that congregations have in forming and shaping faith. This includes intentional focus on developing community, engaging in intergenerational ministry, serving in mission together, and practicing the sacraments of Communion and baptism regularly and frequently. It is through these practices that Christians are made into and nurtured as faithful disciples of Jesus Christ. It is through the catechetical process of forming, educating, and instructing believers that God's redemptive purposes in the world come to fruition.

Reflection Questions

1. What is congregational formation? What practices, activities, and events form faithful disciples in your local congregation?

2. What is your congregation's corporate memory? In what ways are the congregation's beliefs, values, and faith tradition being passed on to the next generation?
3. What is the lectionary and the Christian calendar? In what ways can you incorporate the lectionary curriculum into preaching and worship?
4. What is the significance of practicing Communion regularly? In what ways does it form faith in believers?
5. In what ways are infant and adult baptism practiced in your congregation?

Suggestions for Further Reading

Foster, Charles. *Educating Congregations: The Future of Christian Education*. Nashville: Abingdon, 1994.

Matthaei, Sondra. *Formation in Faith: The Congregational Ministry of Making Disciples*. Nashville: Abingdon, 2008.

Murphy, Debra Dean. *Teaching That Transforms: Worship as the Heart of Christian Education*. Grand Rapids: Brazos, 2004.

Westerhoff, John. *Learning through Liturgy*. New York: Seabury, 1978.

Christian Formation

Everyone talks about spiritual formation, but few take the time to actually define or describe it. We might quickly quip, "Becoming more Christlike!" But what does that mean? Feeding five thousand, walking on water, raising the dead? All kidding (and a bit of sarcasm) aside, if we don't define and explain what we mean, it not only leads to misunderstanding but also isn't solid enough to be useful for practicing Christian education. When we speak of spiritual formation in a specifically Christian context, we are really addressing the daunting questions, What does it mean to be Christian? How does someone become more Christlike? Notice that there is a significant difference between *becoming* a Christian and *being* Christian; they are two different, but related, issues. If our ultimate purpose is the transformation of people into the likeness of Christ, then comprehending and valuing the process of Christian formation is essential to practicing Christian education.

What Does the Bible Say about Becoming "More" Christian?

Scripture often uses imagery—metaphor—to capture the idea of spiritual formation. It tries to capture what may be nebulous and abstract for most people by using familiar pictures and experiences. For example, the Bible often employs the image of fruit to depict growth in Christ (John 15:1–16; 1 Cor. 3:6–7; 2 Cor. 10:15; Gal. 5:19–23; Eph. 2:21; 4:14–16; Col. 1:10; 3:10; 2 Pet. 3:18). Paul instructed the church at Colossae "to walk in a manner worthy of the Lord, fully pleasing to him, *bearing fruit* in every good work and increasing in the knowledge of God" (Col. 1:10, emphasis added). All too familiar to us, Paul's "fruit of the Spirit" itemizes the resulting fruit in the life of the believer (Gal. 5:22–23). Conversely, Jude describes the false teachers infecting the congregations of Asia Minor as *fruitless trees* in late autumn, twice dead, uprooted" (Jude 12, emphasis added).

Another commonly used metaphor in the Bible is physical growth—growing from an infant to maturity (1 Cor. 2:6; Eph. 4:12–13; Phil. 3:15; Col. 4:12; Heb. 5:14; James 1:4). "Like newborn infants," urges Peter, "long for the pure spiritual milk, that by it you may *grow up* into salvation—if indeed you have tasted that the Lord is good" (1 Pet. 2:2–3, emphasis added). The author of Hebrews uses the same metaphor, even including an educational thrust to his assessment of the readers' spiritual life: "For though by this time you ought to be teachers, you need someone to teach you again the basic principles of the oracles of God. You need milk, not solid food, for everyone who lives on milk is unskilled in the word of righteousness, since he is a child. But solid food is for the mature, for those who have their powers of discernment trained by constant practice to distinguish good from evil" (Heb. 5:12–14).

More so, the Bible may even provide insight into the phases of spiritual formation. As previously mentioned, Scripture does use the imagery of physical growth to describe Christian formation, but it also describes the progressive phases of the formation process.[1] First Corinthians 2–3 is the clearest example of this formative process. While Paul refers to the Corinthians as "brothers" (2:1; 3:1), he also describes three spiritual states in which humans exist. He describes some believers as "the mature" (2:6) or the "spiritual" person (2:13, 15; 3:1), while others are "people of the flesh, as infants in Christ" (3:1), depending on their ability to accept and discern the Spirit's teaching. He likewise describes one who is outside of Christ as "the natural person" (2:14).[2] Figure 10.1 illustrates the three phases of Christian formation as described by Paul.

Conversion is the transition point from the natural to the spiritual infant in Christ, and then over time the believer grows into a more mature, spiritual person—more Christlike. The actual pattern of transformation from the fleshly infant in Christ to the more mature, spiritual person is informed by our particular theological tradition—specifically the doctrine of sanctification. For example, the traditional Reformed position calls for a smooth, progressive process of Christian formation, growing from an infant to a more mature believer. Others, such as some Wesleyan traditions, affirm a second work of grace, indicating a more defined transition point between the infant and the mature in Christ. Basically, what you believe about sanctification can

Figure 10.1
Paul's Phases of Christian Formation

cause you to "shade" the illustration differently. But the simple fact is that Christian formation is a matter of transitions, from natural to flesh and from flesh to mature.

A Model for Christian Spirituality and Formation

"You shall love the LORD your God with all your heart and with all your soul and with all your might" (Deut. 6:5). God's words to Moses are later quoted by Jesus as the greatest commandment (Mark 12:30), and he added "with all your mind" to further describe the function of the soul. Spirituality that is Christian is perhaps expressed essentially as the love of God expressed and nurtured through the heart (affective), soul/mind (cognitive), and might (active). The second greatest commandment explains that our strength is to love not just God but also our fellow human (Mark 12:31). We see these same three points when the first gospel message was heard: "Now when they heard [cognitive] this they were cut to the heart [affective], and said to Peter and the rest of the apostles, 'Brothers, what shall we do [active]?'" (Acts 2:37). The Christian life is not just a life of the mind, or the heart, or of service to God and others; it's all three.

The late Dr. Ted Ward (1930–2016) described Christian spirituality as a triangle. As with any triangle, it consists of three corners and the lines connecting them, forming points and axes.[3] Figure 10.2 illustrates the Ward triangle model of Christian spirituality.[4]

In Ward's triangle model, one's relationship with God may reside in one of the triangle's corners, but is more likely to reside along an axis, the line connecting the corners. "Are you spiritual?" The answer could reflect the corners of Ward's model. "Yes, I attend three Bible studies a week, go to

Figure 10.2
Ward Triangle Model of Christian Spirituality

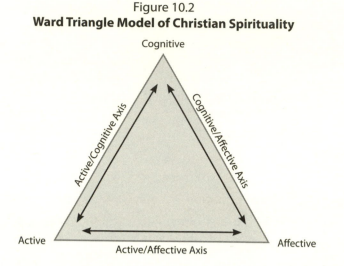

the local seminary for a Bible seminar, and read Christian books." *Cognitive spirituality* emphasizes the life of the mind, focusing on Bible study and theological reflection as a means of forming a distinctly Christian worldview and intellectual perspective on life. "Yes! I spend time in prayer every day, fast weekly, read the Bible devotionally, and go on spiritual retreats every year." *Affective spirituality* concentrates on the inner person, the shaping of the believer's values, identity, and piety; it focuses on the spiritual disciplines and worship as means of formation. "Yes, I volunteer in the local homeless shelter and serve as a sponsor in the next-generation ministry, and also work at church camp in the summer." *Active spirituality* emphasizes service within the church and the community, embracing the principle of James 2:14–18, that faith without works is dead, focusing on acts of service as an expression and means of demonstrating devotion to God. All of these are biblical expressions of the Christian life, not only individually but corporately. Since the church is indeed the individuals constituting it, congregations, denominations, and even theological traditions reflect these commitments.[5] God does not want heartless, sedentary Christian intellects. He does not want believers to be ignorant and inactive but full of Christian devotion and piety. God does not want mindless, ill-motivated Christian service. What does God want? "You shall love the LORD your God with all your *heart* and with all your *soul* and with all your *might*" (Deut. 6:5, emphasis added; cf. Mark 12:30; Matt. 22:37).

How does this aid the Christian educator? We now possess a model of Christian spirituality that is not only biblically and theologically sound but also practical enough to inform almost every aspect of the education ministry. It is simple enough to use in congregations, not just universities and seminaries. Immediately you should have noted the parallel between this model of Christian spirituality and the learning domains mentioned previously in this book. This is no coincidence. Rather, it demonstrates that the education ministry of the church can foster Christian formation. It shows that Christian education must become more comprehensive in the church if it is to encourage and nurture Christian formation in believers and the congregation.

Principles of Christian Formation

What kind of transitions and transformations are occurring in the process of Christian formation? What changes are occurring? Perhaps the most obvious is moving from an egocentric life to Christ-centric living. While Christian formation may compel us to transition along a wide variety of fronts,[6] fundamentally it is the transition from living for one's self to living for Christ. "If anyone would come after me, let him deny himself and take up his cross daily and follow me" (Luke 9:23; cf. Mark 8:34; Matt. 10:38; 16:24; Luke 14:27). In the words of John the Baptist, "He must increase, but I must decrease" (John 3:30). This is not a denial of our person but the denial of the world's grasp on our lives and placing ourselves willingly into the hands of Jesus. "I have been crucified with Christ. It is no longer I who live, but Christ who lives in me. And the life I now live in the flesh I live by faith in the Son of God, who loved me and gave himself for me" (Gal. 2:20).

The personal "ownership" of faith is another part of Christian formation. Writing about Christian formation along the life span, John Westerhoff describes the process as transitioning from a child's experiential and affiliative faith, which is entirely dependent on the parents' faith, mimicking their beliefs, disposition, and practices, toward the searching faith of an adolescent, which eventually is owned by them; it is their faith, not their parents', pastors', friends'—theirs.[7] It is as Paul writes to Timothy: "I am reminded of your sincere faith, a faith that dwelt first in your grandmother Lois and your mother Eunice and now, I am sure, dwells in you as well" (2 Tim. 1:5). Christian formation occurs when we move from affirming the faith because others do to owning our faith because we choose to, not just because someone else does.

Christian formation is a human phenomenon. Earlier in this chapter we spoke of how Paul described the formative process as growth, even occurring in stages, from the natural to the immature to the spiritual (1 Cor. 2). Before conversion, it is Spirit versus spirit; but with conversion the formative process becomes his Spirit with our spirit. It is not an automatic maturing of the believer but one that takes time. Desiring to see the Galatian believers mature, Paul wrote to them as a parent: "my little children, for whom I am again in the anguish of childbirth *until Christ is formed in you!*" (Gal. 4:19, emphasis added). It occurs within us, over time, and as such is a human phenomenon. While you don't need to accept his theory in total, James Fowler captures the psychological dimension of faith as a human experience.[8] As such, faith is not just supernatural but resides within the context of one's psyche.

Living through knowing about God and knowing God marks yet another transition in Christian formation. Our relationship with God is based on knowing God, but it does not stop with knowing about him. We do need to know *about* God; that is without question. If we do not know who God is or what God does—if we lack a basic theology—then it is impossible to genuinely come into communion with him. But our relationship must grow beyond the factual information about him into a loving relationship with him. James reminds us that even the demons know who God is and, given their lack of relationship with him, respond accordingly (2:19). James also speaks of Abraham, one who not only knew about God but knew him, and he calls Abraham "a friend of God" (2:23). While we cannot know God without knowing about him, it is unfortunately possible to know about God—to affirm an orthodox theology—but never really know him. Christian formation demands we know about him and then some.

Relationships are the vital component in Christian formation. "Iron sharpens iron, and one man sharpens another" (Prov. 27:17). In the Thessalonian correspondence, Paul twice urges his readers to "encourage one another and build one another up" (1 Thess. 5:11; cf. 4:18), even providing specific instructions regarding encouragement (1 Thess. 5:14). Christian educators often make the error of assuming that programs bring about Christian formation; the more programs, the more complex and diverse our formative opportunities. Actually, it is not the programs themselves; rather, it is the relationships within the programs that foster Christian formation.[9] It is not the number of programs in which people participate but the deepening relationships within the community of faith that facilitate Christian formation.[10] Jim Wilhoit's *Spiritual Formation as if the Church Mattered* (see "Suggestions for Further Reading") reminds us of this. He writes to counter the wave of individualism that has taken over spirituality, focusing on the church as God's intended environment for forming Christians in community with one another.

Figure 10.3
Formative Ecologies

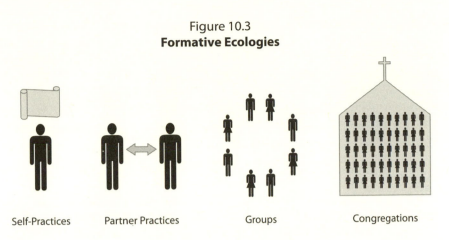

Self-Practices   Partner Practices   Groups   Congregations

Facilitating Christian Formation

How do we practice Christian education as a catalyst for Christian formation? It can provide ecology, an environment that spurs on formative process. Christian formation occurs within four contexts, four ecologies that grow the Christian's relationship with Christ, illustrated in figure 10.3.

Self-Practices

These are practices that can be done by oneself, just you and God. Such private spiritual practices establish a daily routine of encountering God on a personal, One-to-one level. The four most commonly practiced are prayer, fasting, solitude, and devotion. Some believers have combined these by practicing the medieval discipline of *lectio divina*, as previously discussed in chapter 8.

One could combine this medieval practice with a more modern one: journaling, the private practice of recording one's prayers, thoughts, and perceptions as a means of capturing them for later review and reflection. In addition to this, there are more practices and guides to routine prayer than *lectio divina*. Changing one's actual physical posture in prayer is one way of breaking out of the rut of standard prayer practices. The Bible speaks of numerous prayer postures, such as prostration (Num. 16:22; Josh. 7:14; 1 Chron. 7:1; Matt. 26:39), kneeling (Dan. 6:10; Luke 22:41; Acts 9:40; 20:36), kneeling and sitting at the same time on the heel (2 Sam. 7:18; 1 Chron. 17:16), bowing the head while standing (Gen. 24; Exod. 4:31), and standing (Gen. 18:22; 1 Sam. 1:26; Neh. 9:2, 5; Job 30:20; Mark 11:25; Luke 18:13).

Partners as Formative Contexts

Christian formation occurs in communities of all sizes, and the beginning, the most basic community, is that shared by a duo (team of two) or perhaps a triad (team of three). Jannette Bakke identifies three forms of one-on-one relationships that foster Christian formation but require a more mature believer.[11] Table 10.1 summarizes her understanding of these three formative relationships.

Table 10.1 Bakke's Chart on Formative Relationships

	Agenda	Process	Helper Role	Goal
Discipling	Set by the discipler	Instruction	Transmitter	Learning incorporation
Mentoring	Chosen by the mentor	Development	Coach	Improvement
Spiritual Direction	Revealed by the Spirit	Noticing, listening, praying	Prayer, listener	Christlikeness

While there remains a subtle difference between the three, the common element is that it is the relationship that facilitates the formative process, guiding the believer to a more mature faith and deepening relationship with God and his church. Another common practice within these three relationships is the act of confession. Yes, we confess our sins to God (1 John 1:9), but James urges believers, "Confess your sins to one another and pray for one another, that you may be healed" (James 5:16). This requires us to share our lives with one another—with a trusted, mature believer—to receive support, encouragement, and counsel about living the life of faith.

Groups as Formative Contexts

In what possible context could Christians learn about God, experience him in the relationship of the church, and be mobilized to serve in the congregation and community? Groups, ranging from small to midsize, are an environment conducive to Christian formation that can accomplish all three desires. Small groups, also called *cell* or *life groups*, and midsize groups, often called *classes*, *Sunday school*, or *adult Bible fellowships* (ABF), are excellent platforms for two formative practices done in community—in relationship—with one another.

- *Group study*: We must first know *about* God before we can truly know him. Engaging the biblical text, topically or exegetically, with other believers forms a communal context for fostering both cognitive and affective Christian formation.

- *Group service*: A growing faith in Christ is both indicated and nurtured by service to others. We do not serve alone but in the company of others, fostering the affective and active dimension of Christian formation.

Why not have just small groups, or only classes (or midsize groups)? It is not a matter of either/or but both/and. One without the other creates an incomplete ecology. Why? Are they not essentially the same? Actually, midsize groups, such as Sunday school or Bible studies, provide a relation-building step between attending worship and participating in a small group, and an opportunity for community building. They likewise provide a better opportunity to exercise the gift of teaching than small groups, as well as a greater potential for deeper levels of study. Likewise, they are easier to mobilize for service groups than individuals.

Congregation as Formative Context

As discussed in the previous chapter, congregational formation provides a basis for our faith development and spiritual growth. Susanne Johnson speaks of the church as an ecology for Christian formation. She notes that it provides general guidance through what it is and does, and then more specific influence through group involvement and one-on-one guidance until the "church becomes a community of lived faith."[12] And Jim Wilhoit argues that Christian formation is not just an individual, private, and personal phenomenon; it is also a corporate, shared, and collective experience that is part of living within the community of the church. Luke captures the essence of this community experience in describing the early Christians: "They devoted themselves to the apostles' teaching and fellowship, to the breaking of bread and the prayers" (Acts 2:42).

When practicing Christian education, don't forget the educational value of the worship service as formative Christian experience. It is through the worship service, and other large, whole-congregation gatherings, that we are slowly, routinely formed into "a chosen race, a royal priesthood, a holy nation, a people for his own possession, that you may proclaim the excellencies of him who called you out of darkness into his marvelous light. Once you were not a people, but now you are God's people; once you had not received mercy, but now you have received mercy" (1 Pet. 2:9–10).

Conclusion

Why are we practicing Christian education? Various reasons can be presented, but ultimately it is to engage the process of Christian formation so that, like the apostle Paul, we can say that we are "teaching everyone with all wisdom, that we may present everyone mature in Christ" (Col. 1:28). If Christian formation is facilitated best in the holistic nurturing environment of the church, then practicing Christian education is like serving as the Environmental Protection Agency. Practicing Christian education is the means of providing what is necessary, under the right condition, for the formative process to engage and growth to occur.

Reflection Questions

1. Given the Ward triangle model, in what corner(s) and/or axes is your Christian life most present?
2. How does the Ward triangle model apply to your congregation? How might it foster Christian formation more holistically?
3. Which of the four environments of Christian formation does your congregation emphasize? How does it provide a holistic environment for spiritual formation? Where is it lacking?
4. What can you do to engage the process of Christian formation in your own life? What environment could you engage more significantly?

Suggestions for Further Reading

Botton, Ken, Church King, and Junias Venugopal. "Educating for Spirituality." *Christian Education Journal*, 1NS (Spring 1997): 33–48.

Downs, Perry G. *Teaching for Spiritual Growth*. Grand Rapids: Zondervan, 1994.

Hawkins, Greg L., and Cally Parkinson. *Move: What 1,000 Churches Reveal about Spiritual Growth*. Grand Rapids: Zondervan, 2011.

Wilhoit, James C. *Spiritual Formation as if the Church Mattered*. Grand Rapids: Baker Academic, 2008.

Developmental Theory

We constantly observe people growing and maturing, whether it is an infant who is learning how to walk or a child becoming a teenager. We watch as children develop new ways of thinking and understanding the world as they enter into adolescence. We view adults who move from the energetic years of young adulthood to the more stable years of midlife. These are examples of the development and growth that take place in a person's life. The physical growth of a person is much easier to see, but we can learn from developmental theories about how persons grow socially, intellectually, and spiritually. To help persons develop spiritually requires an understanding of all aspects of the human person. This raises the question, what can we learn from developmental theories to understand how people grow? We can also ask the important question, how can we help people grow spiritually? And, how do people learn and grow at different levels of their development? Practicing Christian education with respect to persons of different ages and life stages requires us to embrace insights from the developmental theories. This chapter seeks to answer the questions of how people grow through predictable stages of development and how this growth relates to learning and spiritual development.

Developmentalism

Paul writes to the Corinthians, "When I was a child, I talked like a child, I thought like a child, I reasoned like a child. When I became a man, I gave up childish ways" (1 Cor. 13:11). This is a great observation but doesn't give a lot of usable detail about the process of growing from childhood into adulthood. Our understanding of the social sciences informs us about how persons grow physically, intellectually, emotionally, socially, and morally. Social scientists and Christian educators have formulated developmental theories that illustrate how people go through predictable stages of development. A *stage* is a period of development in which people exhibit typical patterns of behavior. As people grow, they move from one stage to the next, leaving the former stage behind. The process of moving through predictable stages is called *developmentalism*. As a theory, developmentalism describes and explains the general course of development and specific aspects of development over the course of human life. Developmentalism provides a map of God's design of human beings and a framework for understanding the process of human development. Developmentalism affirms the following characteristics:

- Human beings are more similar than dissimilar
- Stages are *invariant* (each person progresses through the same stage), *sequential*, and *hierarchical*
- The patterns of human development are predictable
- Environments facilitate or repress development
- The process of human development must address the five aspects of the holistic human person (cognitive, social, emotional, moral, and physical)
- Development can be stalemated by adverse conditions[1]

There are a variety of developmental theories that help us understand how people grow and develop, which benefits teaching and spiritual growth. A brief overview of each theory and theorist is provided below.

Cognitive Development, Jean Piaget

Piaget was a Swiss genetic epistemologist who studied children's cognitive processes. He was concerned with providing a genetic explanation for knowledge. He believed that children move from concrete knowledge (hands-on) to abstract knowledge as a teenager. In this process, children view knowledge as black and white. As they grow into adolescents, they begin to develop higher levels of thinking, or abstract thinking, which is called *concrete operations*. They begin to develop arguments and reason. This is why many teenagers question what they once believed, which is a natural and needed process as they develop higher levels of thinking. They are beginning to develop formal operational thinking. Figure 11.1 provides a summary of Piaget's stages.

Figure 11.1
Piaget's Cognitive Stages

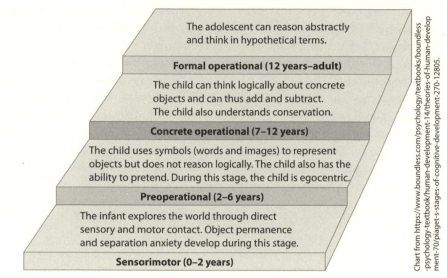

The adolescent can reason abstractly
and think in hypothetical terms.

Formal operational (12 years–adult)

The child can think logically about concrete
objects and can thus add and subtract.
The child also understands conservation.

Concrete operational (7–12 years)

The child uses symbols (words and images) to represent
objects but does not reason logically. The child also has the
ability to pretend. During this stage, the child is egocentric.

Preoperational (2–6 years)

The infant explores the world through direct
sensory and motor contact. Object permanence
and separation anxiety develop during this stage.

Sensorimotor (0–2 years)

Chart from https://www.boundless.com/psychology/textbooks/boundless
-psychology-textbook/human-development-14/theories-of-human-develop
ment-70/piaget-s-stages-of-cognitive-development-270-12805.

The conclusions of Piaget's theory are that we should teach based on the cognitive ability of the student. For example, when teaching children, we need to have hands-on and concrete learning experiences in order for them to learn. When teaching teenagers, we can teach using conflicting views through debates and discussions, which helps them think about what they believe. One of the goals of teaching for Christian educators is to create disequilibration. Just as our ears provide equilibrium for us to have balance, in the same way the brain needs balance. As ideas are presented, it causes us to rethink what we once believed. It is through this process that we learn and develop new ideas. We either accept them or reject them. This is why some people struggle when new ideas are introduced.

Moral Development, Lawrence Kohlberg

Building on Piaget's stage development theory, Lawrence Kohlberg developed a theory of moral judgment. He studied how men (he did not study women) make decisions about justice and what is right. It is important to recognize the difference between moral judgments and moral actions. Kohlberg wasn't looking at moral actions (what we do) but moral judgments (what we believe we ought to do). He didn't believe that our moral judgments need to correspond to our moral actions. For example, a person could believe abortion is wrong (judgment) but still have an abortion (action). For Kohlberg, morality refers mainly to the moral judgment values of right and wrong. Morality is based on what is right or just.

Kohlberg developed three levels with six stages. In level one, moral judgments are based on how something impacts us (pre-conventional). For example, *we don't steal because we might get caught* or *if we steal, someone might steal from us*. In the second level, we make moral judgments based on the community or group (conventional).[2] For example, *we don't steal because we will be viewed as a crook* or *the law says we should not steal*. In the third level, which is the goal of moral development, moral judgment is made based on universal principles (post-conventional). For example, *we do not steal because it violates the rights of others and therefore is unjust*. It is here that we make moral judgments for the common good of society. Table 11.1 summarizes Kohlberg's theory.

Table 11.1 Kohlberg's Moral Development Theory

Level	Stage	Definition
1. Pre-conventional	1. Obedience and punishment	Avoiding punishment; focusing on the consequences of actions
	2. Individualism and exchange	Right behaviors are those that are in best interest of oneself
2. Conventional	3. Interpersonal relationships	"Good boy/good girl" attitude; see individuals as meeting social roles
	4. Authority and social order	Law and order as highest ideals; social obedience must be maintained
3. Post-conventional	5. Social contract	Begin to learn others have different values; paradox of beliefs
	6. Universal principles	Develop internal moral principles; begin to obey these above the law

Kohlberg's theory has been critiqued on several levels, especially because his research was based only on men. Carol Gilligan's critique is that women come to moral judgments differently than men. She calls this the *ethics of care*. For Gilligan, the ethics of care resolve moral dilemmas by deciding what care and responsibility are called for in a given situation. In other words, women make moral judgments based on relationship and values, or "what is good," while Kohlberg's theory focuses on "what is just."[3]

Kohlberg's theory helps us adjust moral appeals based on the student's developmental stage. For example, in teaching children morality, we must realize that they will probably be at a level one. We will have to help them understand that morality is not based on how it affects them but what the community or society says about morality. Also, Kohlberg's theory illustrates the importance of allowing students to ask hard questions in order for them to make morality their own. Finally, it reminds us that we must not rush people into higher levels of moral judgment, and we need to provide safe places for mutual dialogue.

Faith Development, James Fowler

Fowler builds on the work of Kohlberg and develops a stage theory of faith development. Fowler believes that everyone has faith in something, and it can be measured in stages. His view of faith is different from an evangelical Christian view of faith. He views faith as the way people make meaning out of life. It is important to recognize that while we do not affirm the content of Fowler's faith, we do affirm the structure of faith.

Fowler's theory begins by showing that toddlers develop their view of God through the example of their parents or adult guardians (intuitive-projective faith). As the child grows, they move into a literal and make-belief stage (mythical-literal faith). This is why children have an imaginary world. Children have a hard time distinguishing between myth and reality. As they move into higher levels of thinking, their faith is shaped by their peers (synthetic-conventional faith). This is where many teens compartmentalize their faith. They are Christians when around their youth group but not with their friends at school. The goal of faith development is for adolescents and young adults to make faith their own. At this stage, faith is reflected on and internalized (individual-reflective faith). As a person moves into the middle years of adulthood, their faith becomes more paradoxical; they recognize that they may believe differently from others and that is acceptable. They recognize the limitations of their faith (conjunctive faith). The final stage is for those who live a life of justice and love (universalizing faith). Fowler believes the final stage is only for people like Mother Teresa or Martin Luther King Jr. These are people who have lived a life of self-giving love for the sake of others. We often refer to this as persons who have lived a sanctified life of love and justice (table 11.2).

Table 11.2 Fowler's Stages of Faith Development

	Stages	Ages	Characteristics
	Primal faith	Birth–infancy	Shaped by love and care of primary caregiver
1	Intuitive-reflective faith	Early childhood	Imagination creates faith from primary caregivers

continued

Stages	Ages	Characteristics
2 Mythical-literal faith	Childhood and beyond	God is viewed in lawful terms; right and wrong based on consequences
3 Synthetic-conventional faith	Adolescence	The peer group and identity shape the faith of the person
4 Individual-reflective faith	Young adulthood	Separates from group and internalizes and owns faith
5 Conjunctive faith	Midlife and beyond	Awareness of internalized faith and comfortableness with faith being different from others' faith
6 Universalizing faith	Older adulthood	Decentralized self and focus on love and justice

The benefit of Fowler's theory for Christian education is that the goal of faith development is maturity. His theory calls to attention the fact that adults' faith development continues throughout adulthood. As adults grow, they are moving toward spiritual maturity or sanctification. Second, faith development includes struggle and crisis as we move from one stage to the next. Spiritual growth always includes struggle as an important part. Third, faith is reflected upon and internalized in a person's life. Faith must become embodied and owned in order to be lived out by a faithful disciple. The Christian educator is to create a context where students can reflect on their faith and make it their own through mentoring and age-level-appropriate teaching. Fourth, growth through the stages leads to transformation. As a person grows, there is potential for partnership with God and others.

Holistic Approach to Practicing Christian Education

Developmental theories provide a pathway for us to understand how persons grow and develop, which is critical for forming and shaping faithful disciples. Some Christians view a scientific understanding of development separately from spirituality, but we argue that spirituality is one aspect of the human person. A person is formed spiritually when their teachers and learning environment include all aspects of the human person: cognitive, social, emotional, moral, and physical. In other words, our emotional well-being impacts our spiritual life. Our relationship with others impacts our spiritual life. Our spiritual growth includes our bodies and how they function. These examples and others illustrate the inner connection between all aspects of being human and our spiritual growth.

Figure 11.2
Five Aspects of the Human Person

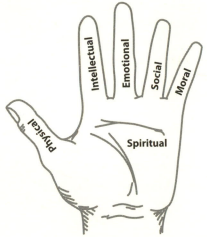

One of our mentors, Ted Ward, provides a helpful way to understand developmental theory and spiritual growth that provides an interdependence of each component of the human person. He asserts that five empirical domains of human development—(1) physical, (2) intellectual, (3) emotional, (4) social, and (5) moral—serve as input and output functions to and from the spiritual core.[4] Each of these components is an interrelated system of development.

Ward uses the illustration of a human hand to identify the five dimensions that represent the human person (fig. 11.2). These five dimensions give us some solid empirical information about who we are as complete persons.

The thumb represents the physical dimension of the human body. The index finger represents the intellectual dimension or cognitive functions, which enable us to think. The middle finger represents the emotional dimension. The ring finger represents the social dimension and our ability to interact with others in a variety of social settings. The little finger represents the moral dimension, where ethics are explored. The palm of the hand represents the spiritual dimension, which is made alive through a personal encounter with Jesus Christ.

The hand illustrates a holistic approach to spiritual formation. God works through the natural aspects or personality of the human person to form us into the image of Christ. Spiritual growth includes the individual aspects of each person, but it is impossible to separate one aspect from another. Within this model we are led to think about spiritual development as the central integrating dimension of human personhood.

Spiritual formation has the same processes of maturity as the other aspects of the human person. The fact that we place the spiritual dimension in the palm of the hand is purposeful. It cannot be separated from the rest of the hand and treated as though it were operating in a different universe with different laws of growth.

A holistic approach to spiritual formation that includes the natural aspects of the human person means that Christians cannot ignore or neglect any of the five aspects if they want to be transformed into the "measure of the stature of the fullness of Christ" (Eph. 4:13). If a person decides to stop growing intellectually, it impacts their spiritual formation. If a person decides not to develop relationships within the body of Christ, they cease to grow. Thus, the five aspects of the human person must be nurtured and developed in order for a person to grow toward spiritual maturity.

Educational Psychology

We can look to the social sciences to help us understand the major approaches to learning and development. Educational psychology helps us understand human behavior. As we understand these approaches to learning, we understand how to approach teaching in our context. If learning is the indication of education, then before we begin practicing Christian education, we must understand how individuals learn. There are three primary approaches to educational psychology.

Behaviorism

This theory was first introduced by the Russian physiologist Ivan Pavlov, who is known for his experiments with dogs. He was able to condition dogs to salivate at the click of a metronome and is known for his work in the field of classical conditioning. Behaviorism was made popular by B. F. Skinner.

The assumption of behaviorism is that human behavior is explained in terms of environmental stimuli. In essence, through behaviorism you can control certain types of human behavior. Behaviorism affirms that the environment shapes the person (fig. 11.3).

A behaviorist approach to Christian education is often used to provide behavior modification, particularly with children or teenagers, for positive or negative behavior. However, the weaknesses of this approach are that it provides external motivation instead of developing internal motivation and that it can be overpowering and disrespectful of human agency.

Figure 11.3
Behaviorism

Environment Shapes the Person

Psychoanalysis or Depth Psychologies

This theory's primary assumption is that human beings are motivated by unconscious forces in the mind. These forces come from inside the person and include human emotions and their influence on personality. Theorists such as Sigmund Freud and Erik Erikson are concerned with internal forces that shape the personality of the individual (fig. 11.4). We are familiar with the statement "that was a Freudian slip," which indicates that what is in our subconscious mind has "slipped" out.

This approach to Christian education helps us understand the human personality and the psychosocial changes of children and adolescents as reflected in Erik Erikson's theory.

Figure 11.4
Psychoanalysis or Depth Psychology

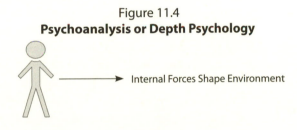

Internal Forces Shape Environment

Humanistic or Integrated Psychology

In this approach, psychologists believe that as humans interact with their environment, not only does the environment influence people but people also exert influence on their environments. In other words, the external forces of the environment of behaviorism and the internal forces of depth psychologies are balanced by our interaction with our environments (fig. 11.5).

The integrated approach is more complementary to Christian education because it helps us understand that learning isn't dependent on our self-perceptions alone; rather, the learner is guided by the teacher, who facilitates the learning process. Educators understand the emotional and social needs of the learner, while promoting a learning environment that fosters experiential learning.

Figure 11.5
Humanistic or Integrated Psychology

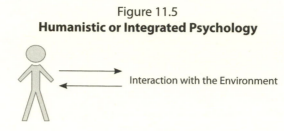

Interaction with the Environment

All of these approaches to educational psychology are part of the content and processes of Christian education. As indicated above, it is important for the Christian educator to understand the strengths and weaknesses of each approach as it applies to learning and development. The integrated or humanistic approach is more compatible with Christian education because it values free agency and recognizes the environment's impact on the learner, as well as the emotional and social needs of the learner.

Critique of Developmentalism

Developmental theories have dominated the field of psychology for several decades but have undergone criticism because of the lack of gender and ethnic diversity in their research. Developmentalism is built on a structuralist approach or stage theory, which is influenced by a modernistic approach. Gilligan's critique of the importance of the "ethics of care" as the motivation for morality and Walker's focus on familial relationship and values provide helpful correctives[5] that focus on viewing morality on the basis of what is good, instead of what is right or just. Also, new research being done in neuroscience is changing how we view the human brain as it relates to development and learning. Neuroscientists are explaining human behavior through the study of neurons and social interaction.[6] For example, we know that the cerebral cortex, which controls decision making, develops much later than adolescence. These developments and others are changing how we view human development. For these reasons, Christian educators have to be students of two disciplines: theology and the social sciences.

Other Christian educators such as James Loder have critiqued developmental theories on the basis of the role of the Holy Spirit, who transforms us during a variety of life experiences. Loder believes that through the power of convictional knowing, the Holy Spirit transforms the human spirit. Loder's focus on the power of convictional knowing is another important contribution to understanding how persons grow and develop across the life span.[7]

Conclusion

Even given the critiques, developmentalism provides us a pathway to understand the holistic growth and development of human persons. Insights into this process assist us in facilitating the appropriate educational contexts to help people grow. God has designed humans with the capacity to grow and develop through predictable stages of life. These stages provide opportunities for transformation and change, which results in growth and maturity. As we journey with people, we will have an opportunity to minister to them during these critical stages of their development. This can include the movement from adolescence to young adulthood or the movement from young adulthood to adulthood. These critical stages of change are places where the Holy Spirit is active and where God can shape and form persons as they grow in faith. Christian educators embrace God's design within humanity so as to better perform their ministry by better understanding the people to whom they are ministering.

We are given a wealth of information from the social sciences regarding human development, which helps us to be more effective in ministering and teaching. These theories in themselves are inadequate for change to take place, but as we partner with God, trusting the role of the Holy Spirit, transformation can take place. The goal of Christian education is to see human persons transformed and renewed in the image and likeness of Christ. We live up to this worthy calling when we work at understanding how people grow and develop to maturity in Christ.

Reflection Questions

1. What are some of the characteristics of developmentalism? How does developmentalism relate to the process of spiritual maturation?
2. How do persons develop in their understanding of morality? What is the primary goal of moral development theory?
3. What can we learn about faith formation from James Fowler? How does his theory relate to Christian faith maturity?
4. What is a holistic approach to spiritual formation? How do we provide educational ministries that address each aspect of the human person?
5. Which approach to educational psychology is most compatible with Christian education? Why?

6. What is the relationship between developmental theory (social science) and the role of the Holy Spirit?

Suggestions for Further Reading

Downs, Perry G. *Teaching for Spiritual Growth: An Introduction to Christian Education*. Grand Rapids: Zondervan, 1994.

Estep, James Riley, Jr., and Jonathan H. Kim, eds. *Christian Formation: Integrating Theology and Human Development*. Nashville: B&H Academic, 2010.

Stonehouse, Catherine M. *Patterns in Moral Development*. Eugene, OR: Wipf and Stock, 2000.

Wilhoit, James C., and John M. Dettoni, eds. *Nurture That Is Christian: Developmental Perspectives on Christian Education*. Grand Rapids: Baker, 1995.

Life Span Development

The previous chapter explored developmental theories of how we grow morally, cognitively, and in our faith journeys. This chapter continues the discussion of human development by looking at the changes in behavior that occur over the whole life span, from birth to death. This is referred to as *life span development*. Life span development considers the many factors that contribute to change throughout life. For example, understanding life span development can help us know why people our age are different from us. Or it can help us understand why people may be experiencing significant challenges in their life. An example is when a teenager is exploring their identity through how they dress, the music they listen to, and the friends they develop. This teenager is trying to develop a sense of identity in the midst of role confusion. Or a college student who is not engaged in significant relationships may become isolated or separated from their peers; they are experiencing isolation instead of intimacy. Practicing Christian education is a matter of understanding the critical moments in the lives of individuals—occasions in which they need additional assistance, support, and instruction—and responding appropriately to those moments.

When Christian educators understand the theories of life span development, it helps us to care more effectively for the needs of the people we serve and to be aware of the changes taking place in their lives. As we minister to all age groups, it is essential to understand how people change, grow, and develop throughout the life span.

Psychosocial Development Theory: Erik Erikson

One of the ways to understand life span development is to understand how our needs interact with society's expectations and demands. It is through this process that we develop our sense of self. The goal of development is for us to have a healthy sense of self: to be self-confident and self-assured, and to know who we are. This is often a challenge, as life can bring a variety of struggles, some of which we did not choose, and others as a result of our choices.

The psychosocial development theory of Erik Erikson provides a pathway to understanding how our ego develops as it resolves social crises.[1] He helps us understand how we successfully resolve these crises through social interactions as we develop a sense of trust in others and a sense of identity in society. Erikson was influenced by Sigmund Freud's view of human sexuality (libido), which stresses the importance of conflict involving the id, ego, and superego in determining our personality. Erikson's theory is more positive because it helps us understand the pathway to a healthy development of the self. A summary of Erikson's theory is provided below, with the implications for Christian education.

Trust versus mistrust (infancy): The first stage of crisis is one of trust versus mistrust. An infant is exploring whether the world is a safe place or not. Infants are uncertain about the world in which they live, and this uncertainty is resolved through the consistent love and care of a parent or primary caregiver. The trust developed between the infant and their parents is then transferred to other relationships in the child's life. It is at this stage that children should develop an attachment to their parents, which is critical for healthy relationships. Success at this stage leads to the virtue of *hope*.

Implications for practicing Christian education: We are to create a safe place for infants to explore their world with loving caregivers. We need to assure parents and guardians that those who serve their children are trustworthy and can provide consistent love and care. Christian educators can also be a resource to parents to ensure they are providing emotional support and care for their child. The attachment of the parent and child is critical for the child's development.

Autonomy versus shame (toddler): As the toddler grows they begin to become more independent and autonomous. The toddler is exploring their abilities as they navigate their environment. The parent is to support the toddler during this process, while allowing for independence. This is a tough and delicate balance. An example of this is that instead of the parent taking control and dressing the child, the parent allows the child to try dressing on their own. If the parent disapproves, it can result in shame, but if the child is given support and succeeds, it builds autonomy. Success at this stage leads to the virtue of *will*.

Implications for practicing Christian education: The Christian educator needs to provide learning activities for the toddler to explore and develop their independence. This means that we are to be tolerant of the mistakes and failures of the child and be affirming of their abilities.

Initiative versus guilt (early childhood): As the child grows they become more independent through their regular interaction and play with children at school. The child is exploring their interpersonal skills through play and activities. Through these activities the child develops a sense of initiative and leadership. Success at this stage leads to the virtue of *purpose*. However, if this initiative is squelched through criticism or control, it can lead to a lack of initiative and confidence. Often the parents stop the child's initiative to protect the child or to punish them, which results in guilt. Guilt can inhibit the child's creativity and interaction with others. Instead of leading with initiative, they become followers.

Implications for practicing Christian education: Christian educators are to praise initiative and leadership of the child in all situations. We need to be cautious about protecting the child from taking initiative and about discouraging or punishing them for their efforts.

Industry versus inferiority (childhood): As children grow, they learn to be industrious. They can do things, read and write, and have capacities to achieve. The child's peer group plays a greater role in the development of the child's self-esteem. The child wants to show their peers they have abilities and seeks their approval. If the child is reinforced for their abilities, they feel confident and industrious, but if the initiatives are restricted by parents and teachers, the child begins to feel inferior. Inferiority is the result of the child doubting their abilities and skills. A good example of this is that if the child cannot develop skills that they feel society is demanding, like playing a musical instrument, they develop a sense of inferiority. Success at this stage leads to the virtue of *competency*.

Implications for practicing Christian education: We need to create a safe place for children to express their abilities and to be industrious. This means we need to provide positive reinforcement of the child's abilities and skills, and be careful to not be overly critical when they fail or struggle. Creating a context where the child can succeed is critical for their development.

Ego identity versus role confusion (adolescence): At this stage the child is making the significant transition from childhood to adulthood. It is at this stage that the adolescent is reexamining their identity and trying to find out who they are. An important part of this stage is the examination of the adolescent's role in society and their sexuality. Teenagers often struggle with their body when going through puberty. The failure of the adolescent to develop a sense of identity leads to role confusion about who they are and what they want to be when they grow up. It is common for adolescents to go through an *identity crisis* by experimenting with a variety of lifestyles related to family, church, education, and so on. If the adolescent is not properly supported, it can lead to the development of a negative identity that includes rebellion. Success at this stage leads to the virtue of *fidelity*.

Implications for practicing Christian education: The development of a sense of identity is essential to healthy relationships with God, self, and others. It is important to provide a context of love and support as teenagers explore their identity. The adolescent needs significant and consistent role models and mentors to provide support and feedback as they are exploring their identity. The church plays a significant role in helping the adolescent see their identity rooted in their relationship with Christ.

Intimacy versus isolation (young adults): Having developed a greater personal identity, the young adult is ready to share in significant relationships with others. The young adult is able to experience an intimate relationship that is open, supportive, and caring, without fear of losing their own identity in the process. The young adult is ready to engage in intimate relationships on an emotional and sexual level. These relationships are often long-term commitments. This can include a boyfriend or girlfriend and can often lead to marriage. Or it could be the development of close friendships among their peers. Success at this stage leads to the virtue of *love*. If the young adult succeeds in developing these relationships, there is a sense of safety and security. If they do not develop these relationships, there is isolation and loneliness, which in some cases can lead to a fear of committing to a relationship and depression.

Implications for practicing Christian education: The Christian educator can foster a community of young adults that provides support and encouragement as they seek significant relationships. This can include supporting young adults who are experiencing isolation by affirming them and helping them to be open to new relationships. Young adult ministries can be of particular help in modeling healthy relationships through support and encouragement.

Generativity versus stagnation (middle adulthood): As adults enter middle adulthood they are well established in their careers and in society. Adults have a greater capacity to direct the energies of their life at this stage. If they have done well in life, they have the opportunity to give back to society through productive work, community engagement, and investing in the next generation. They are generative because they want to share and be productive in the world in which they live. Success at this stage leads to the virtue of *care*. If they haven't done well in their careers or with their families, they may become stagnant. They are stagnating because they have a sense of emptiness and haven't used their abilities to the fullest.

Implications for practicing Christian education: Christian educators can create activities that help adults feel productive by investing in or mentoring children and youth in the church. Christian educators could also provide significant leadership opportunities for them to utilize their gifts and abilities in the church.

Ego integrity versus despair (late adulthood): As adults move into retirement, they begin to reflect on and evaluate their lives. They often judge their success by what they have accomplished in life. If they believe their lives were productive and they accomplished their life goals, they have a sense of integrity. With a feeling of success, they have a sense of closure and completeness. Success at this stage leads to the virtue of *wisdom*. If they have not accomplished these goals and feel unproductive, they often feel guilt about the past, which can lead to despair and hopelessness. Often despair is laced with regret and remorse about how they have lived their lives.

Implications for practicing Christian education: Christian educators can provide counseling and support to senior adults who are struggling with regret and despair. We can also provide new opportunities for these senior adults that utilize their gifts in order for them to feel a sense of accomplishment and satisfaction in their lives. It could be a great opportunity for a second chance for them.

Table 12.1 Erik Erikson's Psychosocial Stages of Development

Stage/Age	Psychosocial	Outcome	Virtue	Description
Infancy (0 to 1.5)	Trust vs. mistrust	Self-awareness	Hope	Develop a sense of self and trust
Toddler (1.5–3)	Autonomy vs. shame	Self-autonomy	Will	Develop a sense of independence
Early childhood (3–5)	Initiative vs. guilt	Self-worth	Purpose	Develop a sense of significance
Childhood (5–12)	Industry vs. inferiority	Self-confidence	Competency	Develop a sense of social competency
Adolescence (12–18)	Ego identity vs. role confusion	Self-definition	Fidelity	Develop a sense of identity
Young adult (18–40)	Intimacy vs. isolation	Self-confidence and intimacy	Love	Develop a sense of intimacy

continued

Stage/Age	Psychosocial	Outcome	Virtue	Description
Middle adult-hood (40–65)	Generativity vs. stagnation	Self-fulfillment	Care	Develop a sense of altruism
Late adulthood (65+)	Ego integrity vs. despair	Self-integration	Wisdom	Develop a sense of integrated self

Adult Development Theory: Daniel Levinson

The adult life cycle has been given particular attention in recent decades due to the increased longevity of adults and the societal roles impacting adults. Adults change significantly throughout their life, just as children and youth do. Studying adult development helps us understand the depth of transitions and changes that take place during the adult years. Daniel Levinson, a colleague of Erik Erikson, developed a theory of adult development focusing on three primary eras: young, middle, and late adulthood.[2] These life stages are divided into external and internal roles and issues. The external aspect focuses on one's relationship to society through social and cultural roles affecting work, marriage, family, and religious faith. The internal meanings of these roles tend to evolve as if attached to a time clock announcing that one's perceptions are due for a change at each era in the life cycle.

Each life era includes a major structural change called a *transition*. A transition period terminates an existing life structure and creates the possibility for a new one to be formed. These structural changes provide us with an opportunity to evaluate an existing life structure and to commit to forming a new life structure.[3]

The following summarizes the three eras of adult development: early adulthood, middle adulthood, and late adulthood (see also table 12.2).

Early adult transition (age 17–22): This begins the era of early adulthood. During this transition from pre-adulthood, the person starts a new period of individuation by modifying their relationship with family and society to transition in the adult world. The primary task of early adult transition is to leave the pre-adult world and establish oneself as capable of financial and psychological independence from one's family. The young adult formulates dreams relating to one's life and work, which is an important aspect of this transition.

More recent psychologists, such as Jeff Arnett, argue for a new stage of adolescent development called *emergent adulthood*. Emergent adulthood is a period in between adolescence and young adulthood during which the adolescent has not reached young adulthood. Arnett argues that adolescence is extended from age 18 to 25, and in some cases up to age 29.[4] The features of emerging adulthood include identity explorations, instability, self-focus, and a sense of possibilities for the future. Emergent adulthood is found primarily in developed countries among middle- to upper-class families, where marriage is often delayed until age 30 or later.

Early adulthood era (age 17–40): This is the time of greatest energy and excitement, while also being the time of greatest contradictions and stress. The twenties and thirties are the peak times of biological strength and performance. The primary task is forming an adult identity. Adults explore choices and options regarding career, marriage, children, and lifestyle. It is often a time of competition in the workplace and a time of high stress. Young adults need mentors in their given career to guide them as they make these significant life choices.

Age thirty transition (age 28–33): This transition is important for most men because they feel that time is running out and that change must be made soon. Many men feel restricted by the choices they made in their twenties. It is a time to reevaluate and rediscover feelings, interests, talents, and goals that have been ignored because they were neglected in their twenties. This transition is not as difficult for women. For them it could be a time to develop their career, get married, or begin a family.

Midlife transition (age 40–45): This transition provides an end to the early adulthood era. Here it is time to measure one's success and self-selected goals that indicate one has "become one's own person." Success is usually seen as achieved when a person sees their work flourish, obtains a certain position or influence in their career, and has obtained a sense of seniority in terms of rewards and responsibilities.

Midlife crisis is often associated with the midlife years. It often takes place in men who have a strong feeling that they have not achieved their dreams. Men often try to look younger through exercise and buying a sports car. Midlife crisis is a time in which men realize that their dreams of youth are a decreasing reality. During the midlife crisis, adults begin to reevaluate their career, family, marriage, and work. They ask questions such as, What have I done with my life? What do I really get from and give to my family and friends? How satisfying is my current life? Shall I change to make it better for the future?

Middle adulthood era (age 45–65): Here adults become "senior members" of society. Either they have a deep sense of satisfaction and meaning in their lives or they face negative implications such as marital separation, quitting a job, terminating a significant relationship, or moving to another location.

This happens because men want to reconstruct a new life structure. They were not happy with the end of early adulthood and want to make changes for the future.

Late adult transition (age 60–65) and late adulthood (age 65+): This period is effected by biological, psychological, and social changes. People become aware of bodily decline and limitations. Aches and pains are more frequent. Retirement and a change of social status impact their relationships with others. Their responsibilities decrease, and financial and social insecurity limit their choices, unless they have planned well for retirement. The primary task is to accept these new realities and to come to terms with the reality of death.

Implications for Practicing Christian Education

As Christian educators we need to ask: Why are these structures and transitions important to Christian education? How do they relate to ministry? Here are some reasons why they are important to Christian education:

- When adults outgrow their era and become vulnerable and open, there are greater opportunities to serve and minister to them. They are more open to change than we realize.
- Adults are constantly reevaluating their lives and addressing big questions such as, What is most important in my life? How do I best invest my time and energy?
- Predictable life events, transition periods, and crisis may provide adults and those who minister to them with a framework in which to evaluate options and make choices that will influence their lives and walk with God.
- Transitions remind us of the importance of relationships we have with adults. They open the possibility that the church is a safe environment where adults can examine their current life structure and adapt in light of Scripture as guided by the Holy Spirit.
- God is at work in the adult's life during transitional periods, and we need to be present with them to provide support and guidance.

Levinson's adult development theory provides the Christian educator with an overview of the changes and transitions of adult life. As adults transition from one era to the next, they are open to receive guidance and direction from the Christian educator and through the work of the Holy Spirit. As adults are seeking God through appropriate avenues of discernment (prayer and guidance), there are great opportunities for transformation and change.

Table 12.2 Levinson's Stages of Adult Development

Stage	Age	Description
Early adult transition	17–22	Primary task is to leave the pre-adult world and establish independence from family
Early adult era	17–40	Primary task is forming an adult identity; adults explore choices and options regarding career, marriage, children, and lifestyle
Emerging adulthood	18–29	A period in between adolescence and young adulthood whereby the adolescent has not reached young adulthood; it includes identity explorations, instability, self-focus, and a sense of possibilities for the future
Age thirty transition	28–33	Primary task is to reevaluate and rediscover feelings, interests, talents, and priorities ignored because they were neglected in their twenties
Midlife transition	40–45	Primary task is to measure one's success and self-selected goals that indicate one has "become one's own person"
Midlife crisis	40–55	Primary task is for adults to reevaluate their career, family, marriage, and work; they ask questions like, What have I done with my life?
Middle adult era	45–60	Primary task is to restructure their lives, to appreciate the good things in their lives, to be rejuvenated and enriched; negative tasks can include job loss, divorce, or a move
Late adult transition	60–65	Primary task is a reappraisal of life; pride in achievements or despair in failures
Late adulthood	65+	Primary task is to confront self and make peace with the world; ready for the last stage—death

Adapted from Daniel J. Levinson et al., *The Seasons of a Man's Life* (New York: Ballantine Books, 1978), 57.

Social Learning: Exemplars (Mentors)

In a discussion regarding life span development, it is important to give focus to the most powerful aspect of growth—human relationships. God has created us as social beings, and we are formed and shaped through relationships. As we have seen in reviewing Erikson's and Levinson's theories, relationships with caregivers and adult mentors is critical to growth and maturity. Social learning theory, or social psychology, explores the way human behavior is imitated from others. In essence we are socialized into families, communities, and societies because of the influence of caregivers and adult exemplars (models). Albert Bandura is often cited for his work on social learning theory. He believes that imitation, modeling, and observational learning are a rationale for a person's behavior. For example, why do we, Mark and Jim, love basketball? Because we grew up in a community that had deep love for the game, and our most significant peers loved the sport (especially the University of Kentucky Wildcats). In other words, we gained appreciation and love from observing and imitating others' behaviors.

Social learning plays a critical role in faith formation. We are socialized into Christian faith through our youth group or Christian community. The practices we develop are reinforced by our peers and parents. We learn through imitating their behaviors and are reinforced in community. There are two kinds of models in our lives. First, there are symbolic models, who are people we see on television or read about in a book. For example, Michael Jordan may be a sports role model. We don't have an actual relationship with him, but he is a *symbolic model* to us. Second, there are *exemplary models*, who are actual living persons with whom we have a relationship.[5] This could be a pastor, parent, professor, peer, or colleague who serves as an exemplar in our life. They model behavior we want to imitate and reinforce in our life. In other words, the transformation of humans is effected through and within the social dynamics of imitating and being imitated. This is often called *exemplarity*. Exemplarity is a generative and productive power for real transformation. Humans are always influencing each other's attitudes, beliefs, and behaviors through reciprocal imitation.[6]

Conclusion

The human life cycle provides a framework to understand the change of human behavior from birth to death. We are constantly adjusting our lives based on life's context as we interact with others and our social context. As we understand these life span changes, we can effectively minister to people in the midst of transitions. The work of the Holy Spirit is actively comforting and redeeming those in the midst of managing these crisis points in their lives. These points of transition can be opportunities for significant transformation and change. The Christian educator also creates a context that supports, encourages, and facilitates opportunities for discovery and learning given our developmental context.

Social learning theory and the role of exemplars help us understand important aspects of life span development. We grow and develop as we imitate the behaviors of role models or exemplars. As we interact with others in the context of community, we are being formed and shaped. This is why the church community plays such an important role in faith formation and the passing on of the faith tradition. Youth pastors, children's directors, and Sunday school teachers are exemplars whom others observe and model their actions and practices on. The Christian educator can help foster effective practices and behaviors that reflect the life of Christ through their educational ministries.

Reflection Questions

1. As you review Erik Erikson's psychosocial stages of development, which stage most reflects your context in life? Which stage reflects the context of the people you serve?
2. What are the primary tasks of the early adult transition? How can Christian educators provide guidance during this stage of development?
3. What can Christian educators learn from Erikson's psychosocial stages of development? How does this theory help Christian educators minister to others?
4. What is social learning theory, and how does it relate to life span development? What is the role of an exemplar in this process?

Suggestions for Further Reading

Arnett, Jeffry Jensen. *Emerging Adulthood: The Winding Road from the Late Teens through the Twenties*. New York: Oxford, 2004.

Capps, Donald. *The Decades of Life: A Guide to Human Development*. Louisville: Westminster John Knox, 2008.

Estep, James Riley, Jr., and J. H. Kim, eds. *Christian Formation: Integrating Theology and Human Development*. Nashville: B&H Academic, 2010.

Levinson, Daniel J. *The Seasons of a Woman's Life*. New York: Ballantine Books, 1996.

Levinson, Daniel J., et al. *The Seasons of a Man's Life*. New York: Ballantine Books, 1978.

Sheehy, Gail. *The New Passages: Mapping Your Life across Time*. New York: Random House, 1995.

Christian Education
and Church Health

Who doesn't want a healthy body? Doctors tell us to eat right and exercise, and television extolls the idea of a healthy lifestyle (even while trying to sell us sugar water and fatty foods), not to mention the seasonal weight-awareness times, such as New Year's resolutions and getting ready for the beach in the summer. No one really wants to be sick, nor do they want to be unhealthy, but it takes attention to gain and maintain a healthy lifestyle.

Yes, all this is speaking of the physical body. But in the New Testament, the body becomes a metaphor for the church, the people of God. Paul uses this body paradigm to call the church to growing, maturing, serving, and becoming what God intended it to be (Rom. 7:4; 1 Cor. 10:16; 12:27; Eph. 4:12). The body of Christ has to be healthy too. But what makes for a healthy body, the church?

Body, Organs, and Cells

The body is an incredibly complex organism. It functions as a whole, but the body is also the composite of organs that support the life of the body and the cells that reflect the health of the whole body (fig. 13.1). When we look at the life of the church, we cannot look at just the body as a whole, or specific programs and ministries, or just the small groups or individual groups that

Figure 13.1
The Body Paradigm

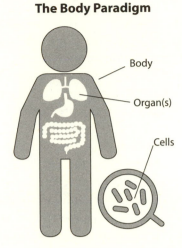

constitute the organs that constitute the body. We need a holistic approach to the teaching ministry of the church.

Carl F. George's now-classic work on the subject described the church as being composed of celebration (i.e., body), congregation (i.e., organ), and cell (i.e., yes, a cell).[1] Practicing Christian education has to take into account the life of the body at the cellular level, the small or life groups, classes, discipleship triads, and study groups. These are the cell groups.

However, cells that all serve a similar or even the same function form organs. Ministries, like organs, are identified by common function—that is, children's ministry, youth ministry, adult ministry, discipleship ministry, and so on. The strength of the body is contingent on the strength of its ministries and their ability to work in sync with one another. All this ultimately forms the body as a system to support life. The body level of this paradigm is found in the large group activities, such as worship services or congregation-wide events. Christian education that encourages and promotes church health has to engage the congregation on all three levels: cells, organs, and body.

The life of the church is found in its missions. We know what the church's expressed mission is: "Go therefore and make disciples of all nations, baptizing them in the name of the Father and of the Son and of the Holy Spirit, teaching them to observe all that I have commanded you. And behold, I am with you always, to the end of the age" (Matt. 28:19–20). Practicing Christian education is building the body of Christ by fulfilling the Great Commission's disciple-making mandate through the teaching ministry of the church on all three levels: cells, organs, and the body as a whole.

Tale of Three Triangles

Who doesn't want healthy churches? Oftentimes we labor under the misconception that healthy churches are huge, with people gathering by the thousands—a quantitative measure of health. Others think that a healthy church is more qualitative, focused on spiritual growth, community relationship building, or fellowship. A healthy church cannot function at either extreme, focusing strictly on quantities or qualities; both are needed to have a balanced approach to health.

In the book of Acts, the church's rapid growth and expansion is cataloged for us in numerous passages; three thousand, five thousand, and then increasing beyond measure (2:41, 47; 4:4; 6:1, 7). Advocates of numerical growth in the church use these passages to explain that numbers do matter and are a sign of church health, but is that the total picture? When we revisit the context of these passages, another portrait emerges. Every period of numerical growth seems to have been predicated by an event of profound spiritual vitality (cf. 2:40–41, 46–47; 4:1–4; 5:41–6:1a; 6:1–7). The context of these passages demonstrates a balance, a focus on both the quantitative growth of the church and the qualitative growth of the church; they are inseparable for a healthy body. The relationship and desirable balance between the quantitative and qualitative dimensions of church health can be represented in a series of triangles.

Figure 13.2
Quantitative Triangle

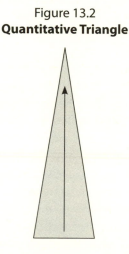

Quantitative Triangle

Congregations that tend to focus on numerical growth as a sign of health are like the triangle in figure 13.2. Narrow at the base, but ever growing in attendance, primarily in the large group gatherings, such as worship or congregation-wide special events. "Is your church healthy?" "Yes! We have fifteen hundred in worship on a regular basis, and we send more kids to church camp than any other church in our district." Notice the equation of numbers to health. While this may have appeal for some, it represents an imbalance in the congregation's body, one that all too often gives too little attention to the organs and cells of the body. With a limited qualitative emphasis, the congregation may also lack depth in terms of discipleship, instruction, mentoring, or other essential forms of Christian education. Even if it has these ministries in place, the percentage of individuals participating in them will be considerably small compared to those attending the worship service. To its credit, it is fulfilling the initial part of the church's mission ("go and make disciples"), but that's where it seems to end. Christian education serves the outreach of the church, but little is focused on the believer once they are there, beyond enhancing the pulpit ministry or sponsoring large group events. Some Christian education might be done off campus as a means of improving the outreach of the congregation into the community.

Figure 13.3
Qualitative Triangle

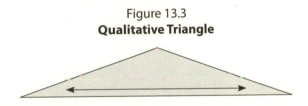

Qualitative Triangle

"Is your congregation healthy?" "Yes! We know everyone there, and we really feel like there is a sense of belonging and fellowship there." There is nothing wrong with any of this, except when it is done to the exclusion of the quantitative dimension of church health. This approach focuses not on the numerical dimension of the healthy church but on the ingathering of the church. These churches are perhaps great at the second part of the Great Commission, "teaching them to observe all that I have commanded you," but not very committed to the idea of evangelism. Practicing Christian education in this congregation would be in the service to the people already there, without an outreach focus; all of the education would be on campus, rarely away from the church building. These churches have little community impact and are somewhat like speed bumps; you drive by without noticing them until you've passed one and say, "Was that a church back there?"

Figure 13.4
Balanced Triangle

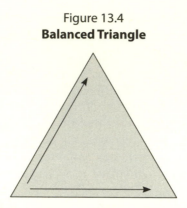

Balanced Triangle

What happens when a congregation is able to embrace both the quantitative and the qualitative dimensions of the church's health? The triangle is an equilateral triangle, equal on all sides. It represents a congregation that has a healthy balance of the outreach of the congregation into the community, a focus on numbers, and the ingathering of the congregation—a focus on fellowship and building community within the body. In such a congregation, Christian education often catches up with the numerical growth, expanding its ministries and number of groups and classes to accommodate the growing congregation. However, what is preferred is that in anticipation of growth, the congregation expand its Christian education ministries and offer additional opportunities for those arriving in the future. In this case, practicing Christian education involves extending the base of the congregation's ministry in preparation for those arriving from the evangelistic endeavors of the congregation. In this instance, the ministry of Christian education provides a basis for a balanced, healthy growth within the congregation.

What Kind of Triangle Are We?

A healthy congregation maintains a balance between the emphasis on numerical growth and the growth of community within the congregation. How can we tell if we are out of balance? Here are a few questions that require honest, sincere introspection.

- What kind of congregation are we? Of the three triangles, which one most describes our congregation?

- Are our commitments more to those who are already here or to those who are yet to come? Are we more of an ingathering congregation or an outreach congregation?
- Why do we not have a balanced approach to ministry? What is it about us that doesn't seem to promote balance? Is it a congregational value that seems to create imbalance?
- What does the community think of our congregation? If we are a quantitative triangle, they should know us; but if we are a qualitative triangle, they might not know us at all.
- What can we do to spark qualitative or quantitative growth?

Christian education is being practiced in all these settings, within each triangle model of a congregation, but with a slightly different emphasis. It emphasizes qualitative or quantitative growth, furthering an imbalance; or it serves to strategically support a balanced congregational health.

Practicing Christian Education and Becoming a Healthy Church

Numerous volumes have been written about the benchmarks and dynamics of a healthy congregation, so there is no uniform, standardized measure for church health. But the following five congregational values can adequately express the essential measures of a healthy congregation, with each embracing Christian education as an essential ministry of the church.[2] A healthy church includes the following values.

Values non-Christians by being openly involved in their community. "So then, as we have opportunity, *let us do good to everyone*, and especially to those who are of the household of faith" (Gal. 6:10, emphasis added). The church's ministry is not limited by the walls of the congregation's building; it must extend to those beyond the walls. The church presents a positive face to those in its community by being an active participant in the community.

Practicing Christian education calls us to get out of the proverbial box—in this case, our classrooms and buildings. If Christian education is going to support this value, it has to provide opportunities for non-Christians to study with Christians on a topic of their own choosing or of common interest. This is not offering 6:00 a.m. Bible study on Leviticus at the local coffeehouse (even most Christians would not want this!). Rather, it is perhaps a parenting group that gathers to encourage, share, and instruct on parenting adolescents. It may be seminars on financial planning, with Christian principles interwoven with the content. It could even be neighborhood gatherings or participation in community events.

Values the gospel by actively evangelizing the lost. If the community has been engaged, some will obviously become inquisitive about the Christian faith. The occasion to share the gospel with a non-Christian will probably present itself not at church but in one of these events, in a more personal climate. It won't be like Peter at Pentecost (Acts 2), but more like Philip and the Ethiopian eunuch: "Then Philip opened his mouth, and beginning with this Scripture he told him the good news about Jesus" (Acts 8:35). Of course, this assumes that the church teaches its members how to present Christ to nonbelievers in such a way that the presentation is conducive to nonbelievers being led to Christ.

Practicing Christian education to promote this value means not only providing opportunities for community engagement but also training and equipping Christians with the ability to effectively share the gospel with those in need of it. It may also produce tools, paper or digital, to aid in their presentation of the gospel, such as an app that takes them step-by-step through God's plan of salvation.

Values new Christians by continually providing for their spiritual growth. Peter speaks of our need to "grow up into salvation" (1 Pet. 2:2). Paul, too, urges the church as a body, saying, "Rather, speaking the truth in love, *we are to grow up in every way* into him who is the head, into Christ, from whom the whole body, joined and held together by every joint *with which it is equipped*, when each part is working properly, *makes the body grow so that it builds itself up* in love" (Eph. 4:15–16, emphasis added). Becoming a Christian is different from becoming Christian. Acceptance of the gospel is the start of the life of faith. Healthy churches provide for the Christian formation of their members, supporting their growth as individual believers and as a body of believers.

Practicing Christian education that promotes a healthy congregation means that there is always a next step provided by the church for the spiritual lives of its members. We cannot afford a gap in our ministries that causes a gap in the spiritual formation of the church. Many congregations have a new-members' class or group, but what is next? As addressed in chapters 9 and 16, a clear path of opportunities for continual growth in the congregation is needed to establish and extend a congregation's healthy balance of outreach and ingathering, not only evangelizing the lost but nurturing the saved. Most recent studies have indicated that new believers need some form of special attention—a small group or class—for about two years before they are ready to move to the next level.[3] But what do they move to?

Values ministry by equipping and resourcing new believers to serve. After two years of special new-member attention, most Christians are ready for a next step, one that moves them toward service within the congregation and/ or a deeper study of Scripture and Christian beliefs. Ministry is not just for the few; it is for all who believe (2 Cor. 5:19–21; Eph. 4:12). Likewise, after being acquainted with the faith's fundamentals, new believers are prepared to grow further in their studies. Healthy congregations are not a spiritual dead end; rather, they intentionally provide not only for the continual formation of believers but also for their entry into service within the body. The ability to mobilize members for ministry is crucial to a healthy congregation.

Practicing Christian education includes training individuals for service within the church. Training is a very narrow, specific, intentional form of education, typically with very precise objectives. It is usually ministry specific; for example, how you train a youth worker and an adult Sunday school teacher may be similar, but quite different in the particulars. Training initiatives should be tailored to the individual ministry and congregation, which is part of the Christian educator's task, as described in chapter 17.

Values maturity by recognizing and commissioning members to lead. The leaders of a healthy congregation constantly have their eyes on the horizon for new leadership—the next generation of volunteers, ministry team leaders, and even those who may be suited for congregational leadership. While cautious about raising people too soon to leadership (1 Tim. 3:6), Paul did instruct Timothy, "What you have heard from me in the presence of many witnesses entrust to faithful men who will be able to teach others also" (2 Tim. 2:2). Healthy congregations in part come from having healthy leaders: spiritually mature, faithful, knowledgeable, capable individuals who can serve the congregation at whatever level they are placed at or by fulfilling whatever responsibility is given them. This is again the example of Acts 6:1–7, where qualified individuals are identified and selected to assume the responsibility of serving the congregation.

Practicing Christian education likewise insists that individuals who show promise be nurtured and equipped to lead the congregation in a variety of capacities. Developing leaders is a vital part of Christian education's contribution to a healthy congregation. Christian educators must be able to assist in the recruitment, orienting, training, and continual equipping of the leadership, working within the pastoral staff.

Conclusion

Here are three takeaways for how all of this relates to practicing Christian education. First, Christian education has to be arranged organically, like a body. It has to be concerned with the whole body (congregation), the organs constituting the body (ministries designed with specific purposes), and the livelihood of cells (life or small groups, mentoring triads, or one-on-one discipleship). It must take the whole body into account when considering the health of the congregation.

Second, Christian education contributes to a church with balanced health by providing an adequate basis for solid growth, not fad-driven number spikes or ingrown, languishing congregations. While growth occurs in all three kinds of congregations (quantitative, qualitative, and balanced), it is only in balanced congregations that Christian education can reach its fullest potential benefit for the congregation's health and vitality.

Finally, Christian education is a progressively comprehensive ministry in the healthy church. It affords opportunities for the nonbeliever, those seeking faith, and those who come to the faith; it even continues to deliver means for lifelong Christian formation and, for those who mature in their faith, training and resourcing in service and congregational leadership.

Reflection Questions

1. Reflect on your home or current congregation. Use the chart below to assess the general health of the congregation based on the body paradigm, with ① being low and ⑤ being high, and then briefly explain the rating.

Body	① ② ③ ④ ⑤
Organ(s)	① ② ③ ④ ⑤
Cells	① ② ③ ④ ⑤

2. What kind of triangle is your congregation? If you were to represent the relationship of the quantitative and qualitative focuses of the church, how would your triangle be drawn? If out of balance, how might it be realigned?

Suggestions for Further Reading

Ammerman, Nancy, Jackson Carroll, Carl Dudley, and William McKinney, eds. *Studying Congregations: A New Handbook*. Nashville: Abingdon, 1998.

Campbell, Dennis. *Congregations as Learning Communities: Tools for Shaping Your Future*. Lanham, MD: Rowman & Littlefield, 2000.

Everist, Norma. *The Church as Learning Community: A Comprehensive Guide to Christian Education*. Nashville: Abingdon, 2009.

Hawkins, Thomas R. *The Learning Congregation: A New Vision of Leadership*. Louisville: Westminster John Knox, 1997.

Teaching for Discipleship

Teaching for discipleship is one of the most significant practices in the life of the church. Jesus speaks of the importance of teaching in the Great Commission: "Therefore, go and make disciples of all nations, baptizing them in the name of the Father and of the Son and of the Holy Spirit, *teaching* them to observe everything that I have commanded you. And behold, I am with you always, to the end of the age" (Matt. 28:19–20, emphasis added). The call of the Great Commission is teaching—to make disciples. What a great challenge to teach! Teaching has always been an important aspect of the mission of the church. As the early church expanded, there was a great need to teach new believers about the life, death, and resurrection of Jesus and to understand what it means to be a disciple of Jesus. The admonitions of those early Christians are still relevant today as we seek to teach Christians today about what it means to be a faithful disciple of Jesus Christ.

Teaching takes place in all aspects of the church, whether teaching a Sunday school, leading a Bible study, or facilitating a small group. The essential means of practicing Christian education *is* teaching. Teaching is central to the life of the church and is a gift given to build up the body of Christ into maturity of faith (Eph. 4:11). One of the primary goals of teaching is to help believers mature in their faith. The gift of teaching is to be nurtured and developed through practice and through understanding models of and approaches to effective teaching. In this regard teaching is also an art. This chapter develops the art of teaching by understanding educational models and approaches to being an effective teacher. Before exploring these models and approaches, we begin with learning from Jesus's approaches to teaching.

Jesus as Teacher

We know that Jesus was influenced by the rabbinic tradition of his time. He was a student of the law (Torah), taught in the synagogues, and invested his life in a small group of disciples. But in many ways Jesus broke from this tradition by engaging in conversations with women, tax collectors, sinners, and children. He expanded the rabbinic tradition to embrace the heart of the Old Testament Shema (Deut. 6:4–5). This tells us that Jesus valued all people.

Jesus's approach to teaching was deeply connected to his context. His approach was more informal and contextualized, and he used examples from everyday life. He used methods and approaches that captured the attention of his listeners. Here is a brief summary of his methods.

1. *Jesus told parables or stories.* He used parables to teach important spiritual truths. Examples include the story of the good Samaritan (Luke 10:25–37), the prodigal son (Luke 15:11–32), and the faithful servant (Matt. 24:42–51). The Gospels record forty-six parables of Jesus. Jesus's use of parables reminds us that stories are a powerful way to teach important abstract ideas.

2. *Jesus used contextual examples.* Jesus used life situations to convey a point. Many of the parables were agricultural because of the time in which he lived. Examples include the parable of the sower (Matt. 13) and that of the fig tree (Mark 11:12–25). We can learn from Jesus's use of contextual examples to connect ideas to real-life situations.

3. *Jesus asked questions.* He used a Socratic approach to teaching that included question and answer. For example, in Matthew 6:26–30 he used the analogy of God's provision by talking about the birds and flowers as being beautiful, so there was no reason to worry about food or clothing. Jesus based his teaching on the important problems in the lives of his students. The use of questions is a powerful teaching method that stimulates thinking and forces people to explore possible answers.

4. *Jesus used object lessons.* He often communicated to his audience through modeling what he believed to be important. For example, he washed the disciples' feet to teach them the importance of being a servant (John 13:3–17), and he had dinner with Zacchaeus, a sinner (Luke 19:1–10). Jesus taught his disciples by example. It is important that in teaching we model what we believe through our actions. Setting an example is one of the most powerful ways to teach.

5. *Jesus used discourse or a didactic approach.* He used a didactic approach
   to teaching on several occasions, including the Sermon on the Mount
   (Matt. 5–8). His didactic teaching approach was very informal. Teaching
   sometimes requires the use of instruction or more formal approaches
   to teaching in order to build a foundation of knowledge.

We could say more about Jesus's teaching, such as his understanding of
the Old Testament Scriptures, his ability to communicate the content of the
Torah, or his ability to prove the depths of human confrontation. These and
other teaching methods of Jesus provide an excellent example for us as we
consider the significant role teaching has in the process of discipleship.

The Role of the Teacher

The teacher's preparing and facilitating plays a significant role in the learning
process. This includes the personal and spiritual formation of the teacher,
the teacher's understanding of the student, the development of the learning
context, the curriculum, and the teacher's role as a facilitator and manager
of learning.

First and most important is the *personal and spiritual development of
the teacher*. As discussed in chapter 7, the teacher is very influential in the
formation of the student when it comes to both the particular content
being taught and the Christian example that is being modeled. We know
that people learn best through relationships and in social contexts. The
relationship between the teacher and student is critical for effective learning
and Christian formation. The teacher is to be approachable, open, flexible,
and an exemplar who models a life of Christlikeness. The teacher is to be
mature and capable of dealing with a variety of situations. As Parker Palmer
states, "We teach out of who we are."[1] Palmer is saying that who we are as
persons is always being reflected on the life of the student. In other words,
for us to be effective teachers, it is not the content or the methodologies in
teaching that is most important; it is the example and model of the teacher
that is most important. As Christian educators, we recognize the importance of the spiritual growth and maturity of the teacher. In essence, the
life and spiritual growth of the teacher is an essential aspect of teaching
for discipleship.

Second is the *teacher's understanding of the students*. The teacher is to
create a safe place for students in the teaching context. This means that the
teacher is to understand the students' development context (see chaps. 11

and 12) and the students' learning styles. It is important for us not to view all students as the same. They all learn differently and often need us to adapt our teaching to their needs. Students have different learning styles and modalities of learning. The teacher also needs to recognize that the students are growing and maturing in their relationship with God, which means that the teacher needs to be available to help them in their spiritual life.

Third is the *development of the learning context*. We know that learning takes place best in supportive learning contexts. If you are teaching children, you use hands-on learning experiences; if you are teaching teens, you use a more informal learning setting; if you are teaching adults, you might be seated in a circle. How you develop the learning context will determine the way in which you teach. For example, if you stand in front of the group to teach, it means you are much more pedagogical in your approach. It also communicates that you are in charge. But if you sit in a circle with the students, it puts you on the same level as the students. In this case, the context is more dialogical and interactive. In education, this is often referred to as the *hidden curriculum*. The hidden curriculum includes all aspects of the learning context, from where you stand, to the tone of your voice, to the size of the group, to the color of the walls, to the arrangement of the chairs. All of this is essential as you prepare to teach because the learning context communicates your overall philosophy of teaching.

Fourth is the *curriculum that is being taught*. There is the hidden curriculum and then the actual curriculum that you teach (see chap. 16). We are strong advocates for following a *scope* and *sequence* in teaching because it ensures that the teacher is covering the primary content that is to be taught. For example, what is it that you want a child to learn from the time they begin attending Sunday school as a toddler until they graduate from high school? How can you ensure they will learn the overall story of Scripture? Often teachers don't follow a curriculum because they want the freedom to develop their own for teaching. The difficulty is that we often teach what we feel is most important and don't cover all aspects of the story of Scripture. We recommend you follow a set curriculum from a publisher, or as a church develop your own scope and sequence.

Fifth is the teacher's role as a *facilitator and manager* of learning. The teacher is to facilitate the learning process by balancing between *content* and *process*. *Content* is the primary material that is being presented, and *process* is how we ensure that students understand what is being taught. Often teachers give too much emphasis to one area over the other, but effective teaching requires the teacher to manage the learning context to ensure a balance between the two aspects of learning.

Pedagogical and Andragogical Approaches

Do adults and children learn in the same way? Is teaching adults simply more of what we taught children, using the same methods and assumptions about the learner, or does it require a fundamental shift in our approach to Christian education? As we begin thinking about the process of teaching, we must consider which approach is best when teaching in our context. There are two primary approaches to teaching: *pedagogical* and *andragogical*.

First is *pedagogy*, which is derived from the Greek words *paidion*, which means "child," and *agogos*, which means "leading." Pedagogy means the "art and science of teaching children." This doesn't mean that it is limited to children; it can apply to adult teaching as well. Historically, teaching has been pedagogically based. Since the teacher is the expert and master of the content, it is the teacher's goal to transmit knowledge to the student. A pedagogical approach to teaching is teacher centered, and the student relies on the teacher to provide the primary content. When we think about teaching, this approach is often what comes to mind because it is what has been modeled for us. We enter a class, and a teacher lectures with a handout or PowerPoint or engages students in discussion. The goal of a pedagogical approach is to transmit the story of Scripture and to pass on the faith tradition to the next generation. Its primary focus is to transmit knowledge from the teacher to the student.

The second approach is *andragogical*, which is derived from the Greek word *andra*, which means "man" or "adult." Andragogy is the "art and science of teaching adults." This approach was developed by Malcolm Knowles as a means to address the needs of adult learners.[2] The andragogical approach is student centered in learning, self-directed, and highly interactive. It relies on the knowledge and experience of the learner and connects new knowledge with that experience. This approach is more discussion oriented and performance based. A comparison of both approaches is included in table 14.1.

Table 14.1 Comparison of Pedagogical and Andragogical Approaches

	Pedagogical	Andragogical
The Learner	• The learner is dependent on the teacher (teacher centered)	• The learner is self-directed (student centered)
	• The teacher is responsible for what is taught	• The learner is responsible for learning
The Role of the Learner's Experience	• The learner has little experience to draw from	• The learner brings prior knowledge and experience
	• The experience of the teacher is most influential	• Students can learn from each other

continued

	Pedagogical	Andragogical
Readiness for Learning	• Students are told what they have to learn	• The learner is more ready to learn to apply to their context
Teaching Methods	• Teaching content that is subject centered	• Teaching that is performance centered
	• Lecture and learning the mastering of content	• Discussion and dialogue

In most teaching contexts, a modified pedagogical approach to teaching, especially when teaching children and youth, is recommended. An andragogical approach to teaching is used for late adolescents and adults, especially when helping them to think critically about important issues and topics. The role of the Christian educator is to determine which approach is most applicable to their teaching context.

Experiential Learning Theory

One way to understand experiential learning theory was developed by David Kolb. Building on John Dewey's theory, Kolb developed an experiential learning model that links theory and practice.[3] Kolb's primary thesis is that "learning is the process whereby knowledge is created through the transformation of experience."[4] Kolb's experiential learning model provides four processes that are to be negotiated by the learner.

Learning begins as a person has a *concrete experience (CE)*. For example, a person works at a soup kitchen. It is through this concrete experience that the process of learning begins. Then, as the person reflects on these experiences, they have *reflective observation (RO)*. For example, it is at this point that a person observes and reflects on their experience of serving at a soup kitchen. Those reflections begin to develop into concepts and judgments, which is called *abstract conceptualization (AC)*. Then the concrete experience becomes an actual idea or concept. In essence this is the "aha" moment in the learning process. Once these concepts or ideas are formulated, they are acted upon; this is called *active experimentation (AE)*. Now the person will continue to serve at a soup kitchen. They experienced it, reflected upon it, made a judgment about their experience, and now they are ready to act upon it again (fig. 14.1).

This process works when teaching includes all four areas in the learning process. In essence Kolb's theory is saying there are two primary ways of grasping information: through either *concrete experience* or *abstract conceptualization*.

Figure 14.1
Kolb's Experiential Learning Model

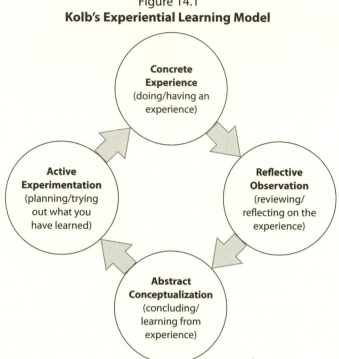

And we process information through either *reflective observation* or *active experimentation*. For Kolb, an experience that is not reflected upon is unrealized learning. Reflection provides the critical link between experience and the process of change in the mind.

Based on Kolb's experiential learning theory, Bernice McCarthy developed four styles of learning: *divergent*, *assimilating*, *converging*, and *accommodating*.[5] She believes that each person has a learning style and that effective teaching takes place when each learning style is included in teaching. This means that the lesson should include a variety of methods to reach each person (fig. 14.2).

McCarthy developed the 4Mat system based on Kolb's learning styles by showing that teaching is a cyclical process that addresses each phase in the cycle of learning. Movement around the circle includes all learners in their natural preferences and encourages them to develop skills in the other three styles. McCarthy's system was to teach to each style in sequence for each lesson or content chunk. For each lesson or content chunk the teacher answers the question most relevant for each quadrant: "Why?" (relevance), "What?" (facts and descriptive material), "How?" (methods and procedures),

Figure 14.2
Kolb's Learning Styles

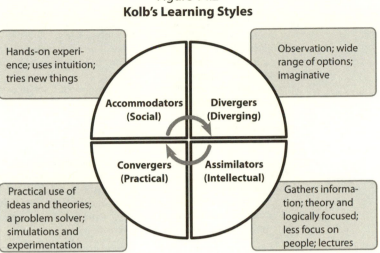

Hands-on experience; uses intuition; tries new things

Observation; wide range of options; imaginative

Accommodators (Social)

Divergers (Diverging)

Convergers (Practical)

Assimilators (Intellectual)

Practical use of ideas and theories; a problem solver; simulations and experimentation

Gathers information; theory and logically focused; less focus on people; lectures

and "What if?" (exceptions, applications, and creative combination with other material). Table 14.2 summarizes McCarthy's learning styles, along with the characteristics of the learner and teacher.

Kolb and McCarthy's teaching model is a valuable resource as we develop a lesson for teaching. The model provides us with a pathway to ensure that all students are being impacted in our teaching when we include all quadrants of teaching. One caution here is that we often teach in the same way that we best learn. For example, if you are more of an assimilator who enjoys learning information and facts, it is more likely that you will teach in this way. If this is the case, you will need to make sure that you give particular attention to the other three quadrants in your teaching. Appendix 14.A provides a teaching template based on the 4Mat system.

Modalities of Learning

Understanding the learning style of the student is significant for effective teaching. Closely related to learning styles are modalities of learning. *Modalities* refers to how students use their senses in the learning process. Four primary senses are used in learning: *visual* (seeing), *auditory* (hearing), *kinesthetic* (moving), and *tactile* (touching). The more active the senses, the more learning takes place. Traditional teaching places a high value on the auditory and visual in teaching, but when we're teaching children and youth, the kinesthetic and tactile modalities are an important part of learning.

Table 14.2 Characteristics of the Four Learning Types

Learning Style	Characteristics of Learners	Characteristics of Teachers
Diverger	Perceive information concretely; process reflectively; are imaginative; believe in their own experience; are insight thinkers; thrive on harmony and personal involvement; seek commitment, meaning, and clarity; and have high interest in people and culture	Have interest in facilitating personal growth; help people become more self-aware; exhibit authenticity; encourage discussions, group work, feelings, and cooperation; and help students find meaningful goals; they may be fearful under pressure and may lack risk taking
Assimilator	Perceive abstractly, process reflectively, devise theories, seek continuity, need to know what experts think, love ideas, and are detail oriented; they exhibit intellectual competence in traditional classrooms	Transmit knowledge, facts, and details; use organized sequential thinking; demonstrate love of knowledge; but can have a dominating attitude that can discourage creativity
Converger	Perceive abstractly, process actively, integrate theory and practice, are pragmatic, dislike fuzzy ideas, value strategic thinking, are skill oriented, like to experiment, and seek results and applications	Encourage productivity and competence, promote high values, teach skills for adult life, and believe knowledge makes learners independent; they tend to be inflexible and may lack team skills
Accommodator	Perceive concretely and process actively, learn by trial and error, are interested in self-discovery, are enthusiastic about new things, are adaptable and flexible, like change, are risk takers, people are important to them, and they seek to influence	Enable student self-discovery, help people act on their own visions, believe curricula should be geared to learner interests, see knowledge as a tool for improving society, encourage experiential learning, and are dramatic, energizing, stimulating, and novel

Adapted from https://www.emaze.com/@AFCQROI/Learning-Styles-DiscoverHowYouLearn.pptx.

As you consider the context in which you teach, it is important to think about how you can engage the senses in teaching, especially for children and youth, since they are more concrete learners. Table 14.3 provides an overview of the traits of auditory, visual, kinesthetic, and tactile learners.

Table 14.3 Traits of Modalities of Learning

Auditory Learners	• Enjoy reading and being read to • Explain concepts and ideas • Enjoy talking and listening
Visual Learners	• Like to take notes • Learn more with media, charts, handouts • Prefer visually pleasing learning contexts

continued

Kinesthetic Learners	• Like demonstrations and active learning • Enjoy physical movement in learning • Like to try new things; very creative
Tactile Learners	• Enjoy creating and making with their hands • Are artistic and enjoy drawing or painting • Use highlighters to mark reading materials

Inductive and Deductive Teaching Approaches

Two other models are reflected in our teaching: *inductive* and *deductive* teaching. Inductive teaching is more experiential and lets students discover learning on their own. The benefit of inductive teaching is that it helps the student internalize learning. As a student progresses in their development, they do not need as much deductive reasoning and information. This approach has been championed by a number of educators, including Jerome Bruner, who believed that through discovery learning students can learn from themselves and create their own cognitive categories.[6]

Inductive teaching begins with very general ideas and proceeds to a more specific concept. For example, you are teaching a lesson on justice and fairness. Instead of beginning the lesson deductively by saying, "Today's lesson is on fairness," you begin the lesson by creating a game that provides the students an opportunity to experience what it feels like to be treated unjustly or unfairly. I (Mark) did this once with a group of junior high youth by playing a game of musical chairs. As we got toward the end of the game, a student who was very competitive was taken out of the game unfairly, which resulted in the student and other students complaining that the game was unfair. The emotions were running high, and when I debriefed the lesson, the feelings of injustice were high. It made for one of the best learning experiences I have ever experienced. The students experienced injustice, which is more powerful than talking about injustice.

The second approach is *deductive teaching*. Deductive is what we are familiar with in most teaching. It is primarily cognitively based and is used to convey information to the student. This approach is beneficial when we're developing new knowledge with those who do not have knowledge of the subject. For example, if you are teaching the Bible to students who have little knowledge of Scripture, it is important to develop a foundation of knowledge before critically evaluating Scripture. This method is good for helping people establish certain cognitive structures before building new ones. One of the tasks of teaching is to help build theological and biblical categories and to use them in thinking.

X Diagram: Inductive and Deductive Teaching

How do we implement inductive and deductive approaches to teaching? Why include both aspects in our lesson? In developing a lesson to teach, we recommend the integration of inductive and deductive approaches because it includes the experiential and the cognitive aspects of learning. Donald Joy developed a teaching approach called the *X diagram* that includes both the inductive and deductive processes.[7] The benefit of this model is that it helps teachers use a discovery learning approach that leads to the development of an idea or an "aha" moment and an application of what is learned to real life. Figure 14.3 is a brief description of Joy's X diagram. A sample lesson is included in appendix 14.B.

Intersection. The teacher begins the lesson by including an experiential learning exercise such as a game, simulation, video clip, or story to intersect with the life of the student. The experiential learning exercise is designed to help the student experience the key point to be learned.

Investigation. After the exercise is concluded the teacher engages in a debriefing process that includes questions about what the student experienced. It is important that these be "feeling" questions, not "thinking" questions. We recommend that you write down four or five questions that you plan to ask. We also recommend that you take time to process what the students experienced.

Insight. The investigation process leads the student to a new insight or discovery, which is often referred to as the "aha" moment in the lesson.

Inference. The teacher helps the students draw inferences from the new insight that was gained and to apply them to life. At this point, the lesson becomes more deductive as you go to Scripture to provide a biblical basis for the idea that you want the student to learn.

Figure 14.3
Donald Joy's X Diagram

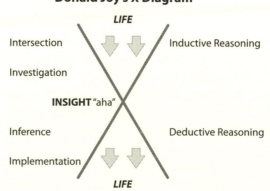

Implementation. The teacher helps the student connect what they have learned back to life by providing an action step. We believe it is best for the action item to be concrete and practical. For example, if you are teaching about encouragement, you can ask the student to write a letter of encouragement to someone at the end of the lesson.

A wide range of experiential learning methods can be used in teaching, but here are a few examples to enhance your teaching:

- Group discussions
- Reaction panels
- Video clips
- Storytelling
- Games, simulations, or role plays
- Case studies
- Debates
- Poster presentations
- Field trips

One important part of teaching is to evaluate the lesson. We have provided an inductive Bible study evaluation form as an example to evaluate the effectiveness of teaching (see appendix 14.C).

Conclusion

There are a variety of ways to engage in the teaching process, and one size doesn't fit all. As we teach, it is critical to understand the content for learning and the developmental stage of the learner in selecting an appropriate model for teaching. Teaching also requires some trial and error as we learn to understand the unique needs of our students and to engage them in the teaching process. With the selection of the appropriate methods and practices, whether pedagogical or andragogical, inductive or deductive, teaching is one of the most fulfilling aspects of ministry. Through teaching we have the honor to communicate the good news of the gospel in order to see lives changed and transformed. We have an opportunity to see students' eyes and minds light up as they discover new ideas through experiential and discovery learning. We get to transmit knowledge about Scripture and our faith to others. The process of teaching educates and equips Christians as they grow into mature disciples. Practicing Christian education is not a static process, but one that has to balance all these factors in order to effectively teach believers of all ages.

Reflection Questions

1. What can you learn about teaching from Jesus's teaching methods and approaches? In what ways can you apply them to your teaching ministry?
2. In what ways does the inner landscape of the teacher impact the teaching process? Why is the personal and spiritual growth of the teacher so important?
3. What is the hidden curriculum in your teaching context? Does it reflect your philosophy of teaching?
4. How do you determine whether to teach pedagogically or andragogically? What factors in your context contribute to the appropriate teaching approach?
5. Based on Kolb's experiential learning model, which quadrant best reflects how you learn? Which quadrant is most reflected in your teaching? How can you ensure that all four learning styles are included in teaching?
6. What is the difference between inductive and deductive teaching? How do you determine which approach to use in teaching?

Suggestions for Further Reading

Joyce, Bruce R., Marsha Wells, and Emily Calhoun. *Models of Teaching*. 9th ed. New York: Pearson, 2014.

LeFever, Marlene. *Learning Styles: Reaching Everyone God Gave You to Teach*. Colorado Springs: David C. Cook, 1995.

McCarthy, Bernice. *The 4Mat System*. Arlington Heights, IL: Excel, 1980.

Pazmiño, Robert W. *Basics of Teaching for Christians: Preparation, Instruction, Evaluation*. Eugene, OR: Wipf and Stock, 2002.

Seymour, Jack L. *Teaching the Way of Jesus: Educating Christians for Faithful Living*. Nashville: Abingdon, 2014.

Appendix 14.A:
Teaching Template Based on Kolb's Learning Model

Topic:_____ Teacher:_____

Age:_____ Group:_____ Date:_____

Purpose: What is the primary purpose of the lesson, and how does it fit into the overall curriculum? What do I want students to experience, reflect, know, and do?

Experience: What do I want students to experience in order to learn?

Reflection: What do I want students to reflect upon or imagine?

Abstract: What information, facts, or knowledge do I want my students to learn? What is the "aha"?

Action: What do I want students to do with what they have learned?

Who? Who are the students in the class? Do they have specific needs?

What? What process of learning will I use?

Appendix 14.B:
Example of Small Group Bible Study,
X Diagram Model of Teaching

Target Audience: Group of ministers

Teaching Aims:
  Cognitive: Gain understanding of a biblical view of forgiveness.
  Affective: Experience the grace of God in their lives.
  Behavioral: Implement words of empowerment in their lives and ministry that free people from guilt and sin.

Pedagogical Practices: Video clip (*Les Misérables*); combination of inductive and deductive process

Exegetical Passage: 2 Corinthians 5:17–21

Lesson Outline

I. Inductive Process

A. Intersection: (Set stage for video clip.) Jean Valjean has just been released from prison after serving nineteen years for stealing bread for his starving family. It was an innocent act with good intentions, but after years of bondage he has become bitter and angry. After he is released from prison, we find him in search of food and shelter. Video clip (eight minutes).

B. Investigation/Insight: (Debriefing of video.) Let's take a few minutes to process what you saw and experienced. As you reflect on Valjean's experience and how the bishop acted, what did you feel?

- How do you think Jean Valjean felt in response to the actions of the bishop?
- Why do you suppose Valjean said, "In the morning, I will be a new man"?
- How did you feel when the bishop covered for Valjean? Were you surprised by his action?
- What did the bishop mean when he said, "With this silver I bought your soul. I ransomed you from fear and hatred and gave you back to God"?
- How were the acts of the bishop like what God has done for us?

II. Deductive Process (Inference and Implementation)

As Christian leaders and ministers of the gospel, we are God's representatives to the people we serve. As ministers we take on the priestly role demonstrated by the acts of the bishop.

Implications: I want to suggest three priestly acts that get to the heart of what I believe to be critical for us as God's representatives.

1. *Positioning toward others.* The bishop positioned himself toward Valjean—he did not use his position of power but instead modeled a position of service. Positioning isn't something that is taught; rather, it flows from the inside out. The bishop's acts were natural because they flowed from a heart of compassion and love that he embodied, and thus he responded in Christlikeness.

2. *The bishop showed his belief and commitment to Valjean.* The bishop was able to look beyond the sin and betrayal of Valjean and see his

potential—that he was created in the image and likeness of God. The bishop's action toward Valjean was one of grace and mercy. It is representative of Christ's love for us. Valjean deserved punishment but received grace.

- Paul speaks about how we have been reconciled in Christ in 2 Corinthians 5:17–21 (ask someone to read the text).

    What is Paul communicating to the church at Corinth?

    What does it mean to be reconciled to Christ?

- All of us were like Jean Valjean: guilty, shameful, and sinful. But because of God's grace toward us we have been reconciled to God. As Christ's ambassadors, by his grace we are able to look beyond the sin and failure to see the potential in people.

3. *The bishop spoke words of empowerment and freedom.* The priestly act of forgiveness is one of the greatest acts we have as ministers of the gospel. Don't misunderstand me—we don't have the power to forgive sins, but we do have the power to release and free people from their hurts, failures, pains, struggles, and fears. And we have the power to say, "You are forgiven."

The words of the priest are so powerful: "With this silver I bought your soul. I ransomed you from fear and hatred and gave you back to God." These are empowering words. As ministers, we can speak words that have the power to liberate people. Here are some examples:

"It's okay to be who you are."
"This isn't your gift. You are gifted in this area."
"As you have prayed, your sins are forgiven."
"We care about you and your family."
"God knows how you feel."
"I think you have resolved this issue."
"It's okay to fail."

These are examples of the many things we say as we live and work together in God's Kingdom. People look to you as ministers and Christian leaders—as God's representatives in the world. You are the priests. You embody and live the words of the apostle Paul—"the ministry of reconciliation." Paul reminds us of our mission: "Therefore, we are ambassadors for Christ, God making his appeal through us" (2 Cor. 5:20).

Application: Write on an index card three people whom you believe you need to say words of empowerment to, and write a card to each person as we close in prayer.

Prayer

Appendix 14.C:
Teacher Evaluation Rubric

Presenter:_____

Evaluator:_____

Please rate the following from 1 to 5, with 5 being the greatest.

1. Was the inductive process effective in the lesson?   1 2 3 4 5

2. Did the inductive process help you to discover an insight in the   1 2 3 4 5
   process?

3. Did the lesson honor all four learning styles?   1 2 3 4 5

4. Did the lesson turn abstract ideas into concrete realities?   1 2 3 4 5

5. Were the primary aims (cognitive, affective, behavioral) conveyed   1 2 3 4 5
   in the lesson?

6. Was the debriefing effective in the lesson?   1 2 3 4 5

7. As you studied the biblical passage, was it interpreted correctly?   1 2 3 4 5

8. Did the lesson compel you to some form of action?   1 2 3 4 5

9. Was the inductive/deductive process accomplished?   1 2 3 4 5

10. Was the lesson developmentally appropriate?   1 2 3 4 5

11. How well did the teacher manage the lesson and learning   1 2 3 4 5
    environment?

12. Was this a valuable learning experience for you?   1 2 3 4 5

Total score ____ /60

Areas of strength:

Areas that need further development:

Leading and Administrating Christian Education

What does it mean to be a leader in Christian education? Why do we have to do so much administration? How do we balance the role of being a leader with being an administrator? These are all important questions that Christian educators face in their roles as a leader and administrator. Often Christian educators don't recognize the value and importance of these roles. We often hear Christian educators say, "I am not a leader, and I don't do administration." It is true that not everyone has the gift of leadership and administration, but these skills can be developed.

What can we learn about leadership from the life of Jesus? This chapter develops a theology of leadership that includes following Jesus's example of leadership and a trinitarian understanding of a team-based ministry. What do we need to know about being an effective leader? This chapter also explores effective leadership principles based on how to manage conflict. What about casting vision and developing a budget? The chapter concludes by providing educational planning (vision, mission, and objectives) for Christian education, including the evaluation and budgeting processes.

Theology of Leadership

Jesus Christ embodied and modeled a life of leadership through his self-giving love and life of service. Jesus reversed the cultural paradigms of leadership, which included power, control, manipulation, and hierarchy. Jesus modeled a life of servanthood by caring for the poor, healing the sick, and loving those on the fringes of society. He modeled leadership by being willing to "empty" himself (*kenosis*) as expressed in Philippians 2:1–11. This means Jesus "gave of himself" in order to reveal God's servant-style power. In this hymn, Paul is speaking to the church in Philippi by illustrating what it means to look to the interests of others and not only our own. Paul points to Jesus as an example of someone who expresses other-oriented love. Jesus's love for humanity and creation is evident in his diminished power and service to others by his death on the cross.

Christian educators start with Jesus's example of self-emptying love as a servant. We are called to be servant leaders who are primarily concerned with following Jesus's example of putting others first. Servant leadership is the principal form of leadership taught in Scripture.

The counselors urged King Rehoboam, "If you will be a *servant* to this people today and *serve them*, and speak good words to them when you answer them, then they will be your servants forever" (1 Kings 12:7, emphasis added), to which he paid no heed. Jesus offered his disciples a new paradigm in leadership with the simple yet profound instruction, "If anyone would be first, he must be last of all and servant of all" (Mark 9:35). This is something he would have to explain more thoroughly to his followers, as Mark 10:42–45 indicates:

> Jesus called them to him and said to them, "You know that those who are considered rulers of the Gentiles lord it over them, and their great ones exercise authority over them. But it shall not be so among you. But whoever would be great among you must be your servant, and whoever would be first among you must be slave of all. For even the Son of Man came not to be served but to serve, and to give his life as a ransom for many."

Those who followed the pattern of Jesus's leadership likewise became servants of God and his church. Paul explained his relationship with the Corinthian congregation as one of servant leadership, exemplifying what Jesus has called us to do in our Christian education ministries (1 Cor. 4:1–2, 6–13). This model of leadership is a paradigm shift in a culture that elevates leaders who display power and authority over others. Being a servant leader is being a disciple. The Greek word *doulos* means "servant" or "slave." The call to leadership as Christian educators is a call to be disciples and emulate Jesus's model of servanthood.

What is included in being a servant leader? We have found the work of Robert Greenleaf to be helpful in answering this question. He believed that the primary role of a leader is to embody an attitude of service. He describes his view in the following statement regarding servant leaders: "Those being served grow as persons; while being served, they become healthier, wiser, freer, more autonomous, more likely themselves to become servants. The least privileged persons in society will either benefit, or, at least, not be further deprived. No one will knowingly be hurt, directly or indirectly."[1]

This is a powerful definition of servant leadership because it focuses on making people healthier, wiser, freer, and more autonomous. And when this takes place, it is more likely that others will become servants as well. A servant leader focuses primarily on the growth and well-being of people and the communities to which they belong. While traditional leadership generally involves the accumulation and exercise of power by one at the "top of the pyramid," servant leadership is different. The servant leader shares power, puts the needs of others first, and helps people develop and perform as highly as possible.

Team-Based Leadership

What does it mean to follow Jesus's example in leading others? Servant leaders are called to serve others. Christian educators, whether serving in a congregation or parachurch organization, spend much of their time serving with others and equipping them to serve. We believe that a team approach to ministry is the most effective approach to leadership. George Cladis developed an approach to team ministry based on the Triune God. The three persons of the Trinity (Father, Son, and Holy Spirit) are in relationship with each other, or are in a dance. He calls this *perichoresis*, which literally means a "dance."[2] This *perichoresis* image of the Trinity is that the three persons of God are in constant movement in a circle that implies intimacy, equality, unity, yet also distinction and love.[3] In essence, the doctrine of the Triune God provides a theological framework for a team approach to ministry and a rejection of the more traditional hierarchical approach to leadership via power, control, and domination.

Servant leaders are to model a team approach to ministry that reflects the example of the equality of the Triune God. This means that Christian educators are to be engaged in developing leadership teams that are collaborative by both valuing the contribution of all team members and discovering the unique gifts, abilities, and passion for ministry of each team member. This includes developing a trusting team. People want us as leaders to be real persons who are authentic and care deeply about each other. Developing trusting teams means we are to spend time together in prayer and spiritual disciplines. It also means that we need to be willing to model effective communication by being approachable and trustworthy.

Principles of Effective Leadership

Being a Christian leader means being a servant leader who develops a team approach to ministry, which is very different from more traditional corporate approaches to leadership. Many books have been written on what it means to be an effective leader, and we find the following principles to represent the key aspects of leadership.

1. *Discovering yourself (self-awareness)*. The most important part of leadership is to know yourself, including what you embody and value, as well as your personality, talent, passion, experiences, and temptations. The first step to being an effective leader is knowing who you are as a person.

2. *Serving a purpose (mission)*. What is the primary mission of your educational ministries? What is it that you are called to be and to do? It is important for educational ministries to have a clear mission to ensure that the ministry is moving in the right direction. This can include the development of a mission statement, along with appropriate goals and objectives.

3. *Developing shared vision (values)*. Developing a vision for your educational ministries requires you to include all leaders in the process. Vision should never be developed in isolation. A shared vision develops as you include leaders in dreaming about God's mission for ministry and discerning what resources God has given to accomplish that vision.

4. *Creating change (transformation)*. Change can be one of the most difficult tasks of a Christian educator, but for change to take place requires the development of trusting relationships and a team willing to take risks. Once a culture of change is created, it becomes easier for continuous change to take place.

5. *Empowering others (equipping)*. Effective leaders take time to empower others by allowing them to use their gifts and abilities in ministry. This includes opportunities for leaders to discover their spiritual gifts and passions (calling) in ministry. Allowing others to lead requires leaders who know who they are and who are not threatened by the gifts and abilities of others.[4]

There are other important principles of effective leadership that we could explore, but the above principles provide a foundation for effective leadership in Christian education. It is important that we know who we are as leaders and that we have the ability to develop mission, develop shared vision, create change, and empower others in our ministries.

Conflict Management

Conflict often results from miscommunication or different perspectives. We often view conflict as negative, but in many cases conflict is an opportunity to "air out the dirty laundry." Conflict management and resolution are needed to develop and maintain healthy relationships. Most of us don't like to deal with conflict, but in ministry, conflict is inevitable. Christian education has its share of potential conflict catalysts, such as classroom selection, curriculum issues, theological debates, and clashing schedules and calendars, not to mention that Christian education typically involves more individuals in the church than most other ministries, meaning there is a higher likelihood of personal conflict within the ministry.

The question is, do we have the skills to handle conflict in order to move toward collaboration and consensus? Here are three steps to resolve conflict.

1. *Define the problem.* Take time to explore and clarify the problem. Often what seems to be the problem is not the real issue.
2. *Generate solutions.* Explore all the possibilities, including the pros and cons of the proposed solutions.
3. *Come to consensus.* The goal is to move all parties toward consensus.

As we address conflict, it is important not to avoid conflict and hope it goes away. The more we avoid it, the more difficult the issue can become. It is also important not to save up emotional energy regarding the conflict. This can result in unresolved anger and frustration that is often directed toward the people involved. And we must be willing to change and to admit we may be wrong.

In order to deal with conflict effectively, we need to understand the conflict cycle, or stages of conflict (fig. 15.1), and our conflict styles. The conflict cycle or stages of conflict are as follows.

- *Tension development*: This is when the tension begins and is the best stage at which to deal with conflict.

- *Role dilemma*: This is where the harmony of the group gives way to the issue of conflict. The tension has grown so much that communication broke down. This is where blaming begins.
- *Injustice collecting*: This is the dangerous stage because it generates negative energy until it is spent, which typically results in hurt or pain.
- *Confrontation*: This is the stage where the air is cleared and fighting begins.
- *Adjustments*: These are the changes that people make to end the confrontation.[5]

Figure 15.1
The Conflict Cycle (Stages)

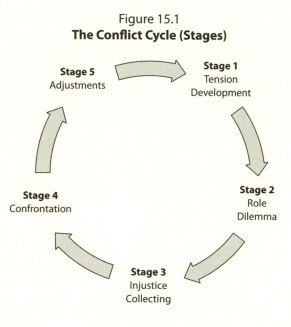

Conflict Styles

All of us have a preference or style in how we deal with conflict. Since conflict is often learned from others, our style can be changed. We can learn new styles and approaches to gain a greater ability to deal with conflict. Our personalities affect how we approach conflict. Based on our experiences, we perceive reality differently than others. Being aware of our preferred conflict style can help us address conflict. Five styles of conflict have been identified by using an animal as a metaphor for each style.

- *Turtle (avoiding):* This style aims to avoid conflict and not be identified with either side. This style communicates, "I don't care enough about the issue to invest time and energy in solving it." The problem is that this creates a context where others have to assume responsibility for resolving the conflict.

- *Teddy bear (accommodating):* This style aims to avoid or deny conflict whenever possible. When it is not possible, the person will try to resolve the conflict as quickly as possible. The problem is they want to preserve the relationships involved at all costs. This person communicates that "getting along with each other is more important than the issue over which we have conflict." Another problem with this style is that the person "sweeps conflict under the carpet" or takes blame for the conflict.
- *Owl (collaborating):* This style aims to achieve the goals of all members involved by safeguarding the organization and maintaining good relationships. This approach gets all parties involved in defining the conflict and in carrying out mutually agreeable steps for managing the conflict. The owl approach communicates that everyone's goals are important and that everyone can work together to find mutually acceptable approaches to the conflict issues.
- *Fox (compromising):* This style aims for each side to win and each side to lose. It communicates that we must all submit our personal desires to serve the common good. The problem is that this approach can be manipulative and inflexible, resulting in strained relationships and low commitment to resolve the conflict.
- *Shark (competing):* This style aims to win at all costs. It communicates, "I know what is best for all parties involved and for the organization, and I am going to have it my way, or else." The problem is that this style is aggressive, domineering, and uncooperative. It distances relationships and increases hostility.[6]

Everyone uses one of these styles during conflict. Sometimes we are a turtle, sometimes a shark. But each of us has a conflict style preference, and in order to be effective in dealing with conflict, we must first recognize our style and adjust to move toward collaboration. Dealing with conflict is difficult, but part of leadership in Christian education is to manage conflict effectively in order to develop healthy relationships and accomplish the mission of the church.

Planning, Evaluating, and Budgeting for Christian Education

Planning, evaluating, and budgeting for Christian education is often the most difficult task for us because some Christian educators carry out their ministries intuitively by seemingly knowing what needs to be done. But most of us need a map to tell us where we are going and how to get there. Otherwise, we wander aimlessly. Careful planning and evaluation are essential elements to ensure that the ministry is headed in the right direction.

To avoid wandering, we establish a planning process by setting direction. The "road maps" used in many planning models of an organization include *vision and purpose, a mission statement*, and *objectives or goals.*

- *Vision and purpose.* In a team-based approach to ministry, it is important to develop a shared vision statement. A vision statement addresses the broader scope of ministry, such as, What will the Kingdom of God look like based on this ministry? Or, What is the purpose of our youth ministry?
- *Mission statement.* A mission statement represents the specific focus of the ministry in its particular context. It provides the purpose of the ministry. A mission statement example is "to teach all ages the stories of the Bible."
- *Objectives or goals.* The objectives serve as landmarks to ensure that the mission is being achieved. An example of an objective is "to develop a summer vacation Bible school program" or "to plan an annual youth mission trip."

Calendar Planning

After the vision, mission, and objectives are developed, then comes the planning of educational ministries and devising a process to evaluate them. In developing an educational plan we must recognize the rhythms and patterns of the activities of the church such as worship, Bible studies, fellowship, and mission events. All congregations have a particular cycle or rhythm of activities, and these play an important role in planning. Other cycles of planning include school calendars, the church calendar, and school events. Such events as school graduations, weddings, fund-raisers, and church-wide events often populate the ministry calendar. Therefore, planning in advance is very important to ensure coordination with the overall church calendar and to provide significant time to promote these events.

We recommend that you plan annually. Most church calendars are divided into four seasons (fall, winter, spring, and summer). Annual planning can take place as leaders gather for a day or a retreat to envision what God has for the ministry. It can also include planning every six months to allow for adjustments along the way. The important thing here is to establish a regular rhythm. Annual planning provides parents and leaders with a sense of security because they know what is taking place in the future. This is especially important given the busyness of family life and work. Some ministries provide an annual calendar or notebook showing the major events scheduled for the year. Other ministries have developed an online calendar for their members to join.

Each event and program requires annual planning and promotion. For example, if we plan a mission trip, we need to make sure to plan a year in advance and have incremental times to meet. The planning includes determining a location in which to serve, the cost of the event, transportation, medical release forms, housing/meals, and promotional materials. Events like this require a variety of leaders taking responsibilities to ensure that each aspect of the trip is planned and that proper promotion takes place.

Evaluation

Many people are uncomfortable with evaluating people and programs in Christian education. Some ask, "How can we evaluate volunteers? We are just lucky to have someone serve. How can we evaluate programs without offending the teachers and leaders?" Just like in business and education, evaluation is needed, and in reality people value being evaluated.

Evaluation can take place through surveys or questionnaires or in a one-on-one or group meeting. Surveys and questionnaires are helpful for gaining information about a particular event or a proposed change. To evaluate teachers, we can connect with them one-on-one or in a group meeting. We recommend that you evaluate all teachers and leaders annually, both to guide and encourage them. We also recommend evaluating programs annually based on the programs' objectives and goals. These evaluations provide accountability for both teachers and leaders.

Budgeting

The planning process includes developing an annual budget. The budget often includes a general budget for the year, with specific budgeted categories such as curriculum, camps, training, supplies, food, and so on. The Christian educator should have a very detailed, planned budget showing the connection to the overall educational goals and calendar events. The budget includes the cyclical programming of educational ministries such as Sunday school, Bible studies, mission trips, and service projects (see appendix 15.A for an example). Once the budget is developed, it is usually submitted to the church finance committee for approval. The finance committee determines whether appropriate funds are available and whether the budget reflects the overall goals and objectives of the ministry. If not, adjustments need to be made based on the recommendation of the finance committee.

Most ministries have a history of budgeting. In some cases the local congregation provides a budget to cover the overall needs of the ministry, but in other cases it may require fund-raising to support the ministries through, for example, scholarships to cover the cost of camp or a mission trip. In children's and youth ministries, fund-raising is often expected, which adds to the responsibilities of parents and leaders.

Financial management and budgeting demonstrate the Christian educator's ability to be a good steward of ministry. A system should be created to ensure that receipts for purchases are saved, records are maintained, and money is handled wisely. When possible, Christian educators should not be in charge of handling money. Monies should be handled by two or more people to ensure accountability. Too many ministers have lost their jobs and ministries because of the inappropriate handling of money. Having a system of accountability ensures confidentiality and protection of the ministry.

Conclusion

Leading in Christian education includes following Jesus's example of being a servant leader. Being a servant leader is contrary to more traditional forms of leadership that focus on power and control. Servant leaders recognize the importance of self-emptying love through a life of service to others. This kind of leader embodies a team approach to ministry that values and empowers others' gifts and abilities. A team approach to leading means that everyone has equal value and is called to live and serve in relationship with each other. To lead effectively we need to understand ourselves, develop a shared vision, and equip others for service.

Leadership also includes planning, evaluation, and budgeting as important administrative aspects of ministry. Some Christian educators don't always see the value of these tasks, but effective planning provides the ministry with a road map to follow with a clear direction. The planning provides an opportunity for the map to be evaluated to ensure that the goals and objectives are being achieved. And the budgetary process gives the Christian educator the necessary resources to drive the calendar of events. All of these planning processes are necessary for Christian educators to carry out the mission and call to develop disciples.

Reflection Questions

1. What does it mean to embody leadership as reflected in Jesus's example of leadership?
2. What are the theological bases for a team approach to leadership? What are the inherent challenges in developing a team approach to leadership?
3. In reviewing the principles of effective leadership, what aspects do you find yourself doing well, and what aspects need further development?
4. What is your preferred style of conflict management? What aspects of your approach to conflict management need to change?
5. Why is it important to plan, evaluate, and budget in Christian education? What aspects of the planning process are you doing well, and what aspects need improvement?
6. Does your Christian educational ministry have a clearly defined vision, mission, and objectives?

Suggestions for Further Reading

Anthony, Michael, and James Riley Estep Jr., eds. *Managing Essentials for Christian Ministries.* Nashville: B&H Academic, 2005.

Carroll, Jackson W. *As One with Authority: Reflective Leadership in Ministry.* Louisville: Westminster John Knox, 1991.

Cladis, George. *Leading the Team-Based Church: How Pastors and Church Staffs Can Grow Together into a Powerful Fellowship of Leaders.* San Francisco: Jossey-Bass, 1999.

Fraker, Anne T., and Larry C. Spears, eds. *Seeker and Servant: Reflections on Religious Leadership; The Private Writings of Robert K. Greenleaf.* San Francisco: Jossey-Bass, 1996.

Kouzes, James M., and Barry Z. Posner. *Christian Reflections on the Leadership Challenge.* San Francisco: Jossey-Bass, 2006.

McNeal, Reggie. *Practicing Greatness: Seven Disciplines of Extraordinary Spiritual Leaders.* San Francisco: Jossey-Bass, 2006.

Appendix 15.A:
Christian Education Budget Template

	Projected Budget	Actual Expenses
Sunday School Curriculum		
• Preschool		
• Elementary		
• Youth		
• Adults		
Wednesday Night Youth Group		
Wednesday Night Children's Program		
Parents' Meetings		
Vacation Bible Study		
Mission Trips		
Teacher/Leadership Training		
Preschool Programming/Materials		
Elementary Programming/Materials		
Youth Programming/Materials		
Young Adult/Singles Programming/Materials		
Adult Programming/Materials		
Refreshments		
Supplies (Paper, Pencils, Crayons, Tape, Etc.)		
Educational Media Equipment		
Library Resources		
Reference Materials (Bible, Concordances, Etc.)		
Retreats		
Summer Camps		
Transportation		
Background Checks		
Total Budget		

Adapted from www.umcdiscipleship.org/downloads/force?entry_id=2806.

A Path toward Spiritual Maturity: Curriculum

For far too many Christian educators, *curriculum* conjures images of packages received from publishers that contain a quarter's lesson plans, along with a lot of handouts, wall charts, and a student book. For others, it may be a DVD or flash drive accompanied by a leader's guide and participant booklets, following the deadly motto, "If you can read, you can lead." Curriculum is actually far more important, should be more influential, and represents everything from the metanarrative of Christian education in your congregation all the way down to what is occurring in every session of small groups, classes, training sessions, and whatever else may constitute your Christian education ministry. Practicing Christian education requires not only a map but also directions for the journey. That is the curriculum.[1]

The Latin root of *curriculum*, *currere*, literally means "to run," like a runner on a track. Hence it came to mean the course of study, the track the student would follow from beginning to end. This is why the word can be used to describe everything from the packet of materials purchased from a publishing company to the intentional learning experiences of a congregation. The curriculum is like a *prescription*, a prescribed track, what you should learn.[2] It is about both who should learn what and how they should learn it. James Plueddemann's seminal question "Do we teach the Bible or do we teach students?" reflects these two basic curriculum questions.[3] Reflecting back on chapter 10, the three basic forms of objectives (cognitive, affective, and behavioral) integrate with one another, providing a comprehensive learning experience for believers. Therefore, learning experiences can be a path toward discipleship; "the curriculum, as a key or instrument of education, must guide the learner to be and become a 'response-able' disciple of Jesus Christ."[4] Curriculum is a practical tool in the hands of a Christian educator, just as a map, compass, and destination are essential for the explorer. The real question is, are we using it or are we neglecting it?

You Can't Teach Everything

Every church has a curriculum. The question is, how aware is the church of it and is the church making constructive use of it? We know what we want people to learn, either directly or indirectly, as well as what we choose not to teach. In curricular terms, this includes the *explicit*, the *hidden*, and the *null* curriculum (fig. 16.1). The *explicit* curriculum is the directly stated information about the curriculum, such as when a church seminar openly states the content and the intended learning objectives. It is what the Christian educator says you should learn from this class, seminar, or group. Because it is the most visible, outer layer of the curriculum, many assume it is the *only* layer of the curriculum; but there are actually two more layers.

Figure 16.1
Three Curricula

The *hidden* or implicit curriculum is what is intentionally taught, but *indirectly*, not explicitly. It is what is learned in addition to what is explicitly taught. It is what you learn by participating in the educational setting somewhat indirectly, apart from the intentional instruction. For example, if you are a very punctual person, rarely late with anything, perhaps you learned punctuality not from the explicit curriculum of a seminary class but by being in a class wherein the professor would not accept late work. Hidden curriculum is what individuals are intended to learn *beyond* the explicit curriculum.

The *null* curriculum dwarfs the others. You cannot teach everything, and this curriculum is null because it is composed of all that was intentionally omitted. The reason for the omissions may be theology, tradition, church practice, the intellectual or faith level of the learner, the teacher's lack of knowledge on the subject, or that what was omitted could not be covered in the available time.[5] Ironically, the null curriculum is what the learner is not supposed to know; it's the curriculum's black box. Practicing Christian education engages all three curricula in the church. Whether consciously or unconsciously, by plan or not, we operate with a curriculum in our ministry.

Curriculum can be misunderstood as boring. Classes and groups, lesson plan packets, learning aids and materials, and outlines of content with ac-companying teaching methods, not to mention assessments, don't necessarily excite anyone. However, thinking of curriculum in that fashion is like describ-ing a vacation as cars, tires, gas stations, en-route hotel reservations, maps or GPS, and road signs. Boring? Described like that, it would be. However, the destination makes it worth the effort. Curriculum in the church is our road map toward discipleship, Christian formation, and a vibrant faith within the church. D. Campbell Wyckoff captures this best, writing, "The task of Christian education is the nurture of the Christian life. In order that such nurture may be effective in accomplishing its purpose, the church as a rule rejects reliance upon haphazard means and adopts a reasoned and planned teaching-learning process for its education work. A curriculum is a plan by which the teaching-learning process may be systematically undertaken."[6]

Practicing Christian education requires us to design curriculum. As Chris-tian educators, we are responsible for providing the road map, the next steps in the spiritual pilgrimage.

Thinking Curricularly about Ministry

Typically we think of lesson plans as individual, stand-alone, usually indepen-dent lesson plans. Real curriculum planning requires an opposite process, one that starts not with writing lesson aims but with looking more broadly at learning in the church or the specific education ministry in which we serve. Figure 16.2 illustrates the four levels of thinking required for a comprehensive, disciple-making curriculum: purpose, objectives, goals, and aims.

While writing a lesson plan for children's church, youth group, or Sunday school may start with a lesson aim, curriculum requires us to do the opposite. Reflective of the mission of the church, or of your own specific education ministry, what is the church's or ministry's *purpose*? In a sentence or two, how would you explain why you are doing this ministry, program, or study? Purpose arises from theological convictions, from the congregation's mission, and from understanding the overarching needs of believers. For example, if

Figure 16.2
Purpose, Objectives, Goals, and Aims

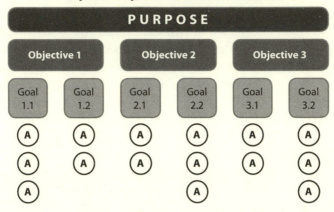

someone participated in the youth group or small group ministry for three years, generally speaking, what would change about them from the time they entered the ministry? That's the purpose. It's why you are doing it. Just as when Google Earth starts by showing the planet Earth at a distance and then spins slowly toward the requested location, before you start writing lesson plans, get your bearings by thinking of the overarching, big-picture purpose of the lesson.

Objectives break the purpose down into more tangible, sometimes measurable components. Like an exegetical paper, they often are an itemized explanation of the curriculum's purpose. Returning to our map analogy using Google Earth, the earth spins on the webpage to the continent before zooming into the desired location. If the purpose is a broad, general statement seemingly impossible to accomplish in a single educational endeavor, the objectives break it down into more manageable components that can be more readily addressed. Depending on the curriculum's purpose, the objectives may reflect the learning domains: cognitive, affective, and/or volitional. These arise from a more precise categorizing of the desired learning.

Depending on the size of the curriculum, subject matter, or duration of the study, objectives may be delineated further with *goals* (plural) associated with each of the objectives. These become even more measurable components, each one related back to a particular objective. If we use Google Earth's more practical application, Google Maps, goals are the part of the directions that show the entire travel path in a basic line-map from point A to point B. Like objectives, goals are more measurable and are an explanation, a domain-specific, measurable learning goal.

But what about the turn-by-turn directions? That's the part with which we are most familiar. *Aims* are the intended outcomes of individual lessons, with multiple aims further supporting the goal with which the aim is affiliated. "Turn right in 100 feet, and then in 200 feet, turn left . . ."; a lesson aim is a very narrow, often singular, measurable, stated learning outcome. Lesson aims are the single steps along the curriculum path that move us through the goals and objectives toward reaching the purpose of the whole curriculum.

Curriculum Examples

What if the *purpose* of an adult Bible study is to become a people of prayer? That's a broad statement of intent—far too broad to give significant direction to what each class session should contain. The *objectives* of the curriculum break down its intent further, such as follows:

Objective 1: Participants will understand prayer better (cognitive)
Objective 2: Participants will value prayer more (affective)
Objective 3: Participants will practice prayer more often (active)

It is not always necessary to have an objective from each of the learning domains, but in this case it aids the example. The objectives give further direction to the curriculum, but there must be further delineation for Christian education to really inform lesson aims. The *goals* of the curriculum further delineate the objectives. For example:

Objective 1: Participants will understand prayer better (cognitive)
Goal 1.1: Prayer in the Old Testament
Goal 1.2: Prayer in the New Testament
Goal 1.3: A theology of prayer

Objective 2: Participants will value prayer more (affective)
Goal 2.1: Participants will experience different kinds of prayer
Goal 2.2: Participants will know the value of prayer

Objective 3: Participants will practice prayer more often (active)
Goal 3.1: Prayer as a spiritual discipline (e.g., *lectio divina*)
Goal 3.2: Prayer postures and practices

Notice how the goals break out the intent of the learning objective into more specific areas of study, but always relate back to the objective, which in turn relates back to the purpose of the class's study. What about the *aims*? Under each goal will be the lesson plan(s) (often plural) for each class session or gathering. Each time, a lesson will be used with an aim of focusing on the intended, most specific learning outcome. For example, Goal 1.2 might have three lessons associated with it, such as follows:

Objective 1: Participants will understand prayer better (cognitive)

Goal 1.2: Prayer in the New Testament

> *Aim 1.2.1*: Students will be able to explain the prayer practices of Jesus as described in the Gospels
>
> *Aim 1.2.2*: Students will be able to describe the role of prayer in the book of Acts
>
> *Aim 1.2.3*: Students will know the different uses of prayer from Paul's Epistles and the General Epistles

Each lesson aim builds upon the other aim(s) to support a learning goal, which in turn supports an objective, all culminating in the fulfillment of the class's purpose in studying prayer. Without such a road map for study, learning is hit-or-miss, and you may not even know whether it is on target, since without a curriculum there are no right or wrong directions to take—you're just teaching to be teaching, not knowing what to expect around the next corner. Practicing Christian education requires Christian educators to think of not only the individual class session, wherein the lesson plan with its aim will guide the hour of study, but also the more encompassing context of the purpose, objectives, and goals that the lesson aim supports. If not, the answer to "What should we learn after three years in our Bible study?" is a disappointing "At best, 156 hours of lessons with no intentional, predetermined cumulative learning effect."

Doing Curriculum Supervision

The principal question of curriculum supervision is who makes the curricular decisions. Typically, the Christian educator is the lead person in the process of planning the curriculum of the church—but they are not the only person whose voice needs to be heard in this regard. Determining the purpose, objectives, goals, and sometimes even the lesson aims of a program, class study, or group dialogue is often not the sole property of the Christian educator but includes some of those affected by the decision itself—that is, teachers, sponsors, facilitators, and volunteers. Curriculum supervision is a collective process that can become a catalyst for improvement and innovation.[7] But what items require supervision?

First, determine the content's scope and sequence. Once Christian educators and/or their team decide on the content, two rudimentary decisions must still be made about the content. *Scope* refers to how much of the content can actually be covered. Limiting factors like the time given for instruction, setting, age-appropriate concerns, learning capabilities of the students, and even support resources affect what parts of the content are actually covered in the curriculum. This is the scope of the curriculum. Of course, if one sets the desired scope, often some of the limiting factors can be removed or addressed. But in what order should the content be covered, and how much should be covered in each session? This is *sequence*. It may be determined by chronology or common themes, or move from the part to the whole or from the whole to the part. The sequence serves as the rationale for the structure of the content in the curriculum.

Second, select the most effective organization of material. Leroy Ford describes three basic ways of organizing the curriculum's content.[8] (1) The *anchor model* uses a common topic or theme to anchor the content, while goals or lesson aims are relatively independent of one another. If the objective serves as an anchor, then the goals, while independent of one another, are connected by a common theme. (2) The *linear model* differs from the anchor in that each goal or lesson aim builds on the previous one; it is a progressive arrangement that must be taken in order to have its full effect. In this instance, it is not just a common theme that organizes the curriculum but the intentional relationship of the content that builds upon the previous material and will be built upon by the next one. (3) Finally, the *wheel model* provides several advantages. As with the other models, a common theme serves to unify the content, but while the lessons are not progressively sequential, meaning they have to be taken in order, they do relate to one another, so they are interdependent. As the curriculum specialist, the Christian educator will need to determine which model best fits the formation of objectives, goals, and/or lesson aims in the curriculum.

Third, develop resources in support of the curriculum. Churches and their ministries do not have unlimited resources. Managing resources to maintain and advance the curriculum is crucial for a vibrant ministry of education. Resources such as personnel, finances, teaching/learning aids, technology, and learning resources for volunteers all support the congregation's curriculum. This often requires policies and procedures to be established as part of the supervision of curriculum, especially in regard to the appropriate use of financial resources and personnel.

Fourth, establish a basic means of assessing curriculum. Many Christian educators shy away from assessment, even of curriculum. However, a lack of assessment leads to chronic, long-term weakness in the curriculum, meaning it's not going to transform participants and make them into disciples as hoped and expected. Without oversimplifying the matter, it is really a three-step process.

1. *What was the desired outcome?* In this case, we can assess aims, goals, objectives, and even the purpose statements, since all of them are statements of anticipated outcomes.
2. *What was the actual outcome?* To assess is to evaluate how something actually functions—not just what it is supposed to do but what it actually does.
3. *How do the two compare?* How did the curriculum's actual performance compare with the desired or anticipated performance? Did it measure up?

This process does require the Christian educator to ask some very straightforward questions, often in the form of a survey or a conversation with people in the group or class. Surveys are often used to gather quantitative data—that is, numbers. They ask someone, for example, "On a scale of 1 to 5 do you feel . . ." and then use some basic statistics to calculate the average response. Interviews or focus groups are the most common means of gathering qualitative data—that is, information in the form of words, not numbers. Asking a class about their curriculum or a small group about the DVD series and writing down their impressions is a good way to assess the curriculum's actual performance and the teacher's abilities. Using both quantitative and qualitative methods is best for accurately measuring the curriculum's performance.

Maximizing the Use of Prepackaged Curriculum

Most Christian educators and their ministries still rely heavily on prepackaged curriculum—packets of materials, DVDs with student booklets, or a subscription to a streaming curriculum service with downloadable PDF handouts. These prepackaged curriculum pieces are typically of a high quality and are an invaluable resource to the education ministry, since they bring expertise and ease of use and save volunteers time. However, just like clothes purchased off the rack, they are not tailored to fit, and the content is likewise generic since it was designed for a general audience and not your specific congregation.

Most congregations need to rely on prepackaged curriculum because they do not have a Christian educator on their ministry staff, nor do volunteers have the time or expertise to develop their own curriculum. But what are some ways the church can make the most effective use of packaged curriculum, maximizing its learning potential? First, teachers can be instructed on the use of curriculum, helping them simply be more familiar with what is in it and walking them through how to use it. Second, the packaged curriculum could be supplemented: used as the basis of teaching but with other activities or materials added to it. Different learning activities or even a deeper Bible study could be prepared, with the original prepackaged curriculum as the basis. Third, while it may not be suitable for more advanced study, prepackaged curriculum could be used for more basic levels of study, perhaps for new believers or even nonbelievers. Remember, it is not made to fit every situation or congregation, but in the hands of an equipped and trained teacher, it can be used effectively in the group or class.

Conclusion

Every Christian educator, ministry of education, and congregation has a curriculum. But the degree to which that curriculum can be articulated, or the degree to which we intentionally make use of it in developing the Christian education ministry, becomes the real question. Curriculum development may seem tedious and even unnecessary, but practicing Christian education requires that we articulate the purpose, objectives, goals, and aims of the congregation, the ministry, or even the programs that comprise our ministry.

Reflection Questions

1. Does your congregation provide a path to maturity with an explicit curriculum? Why or why not?

2. What is your congregation's explicit curriculum? Hidden? Null? How would you know it's null?

3. On a scale of 1 to 5 (1 being low, 5 being high), how would you rate the curriculum supervision in your congregation?

4. How does your church use prepackaged curriculum?

Suggestions for Further Reading

Ellis, Arthur K. *Exemplars of Curriculum Theory*. Larchmont, NY: Eyes on Education, 2004.

Estep, James Riley, Jr., Roger White, and Karen Estep. *Mapping Out Curriculum in Your Church*. Nashville: B&H, 2011.

Harris, Maria. *Fashion Me a People: Curriculum in the Church*. Louisville: Westminster John Knox, 1989.

Wyckoff, D. Campbell. *Theory and Design of Christian Education Curriculum*. Philadelphia: Westminster, 1961.

Equipping for Service

"Why waste time training others to do what I already know how to do?" You just placed yourself in the same shoes as Moses in Exodus 18 and the apostles in Acts 6. In both cases, their God-given mission was thwarted by their inability to delegate, to share the responsibility, to equip and resource others to become part of the ministry of God's people. Ministry was meant to be shared by the many, not hoarded by the few. "And he gave the apostles, the prophets, the evangelists, the shepherds and teachers," why, for what purpose? "*To equip the saints* for the work of ministry, for building up the body of Christ" (Eph. 4:11–12, emphasis added). Moses could not do it all himself. The apostles could not do it all themselves. Paul admonishes the church at Ephesus to realize that those who are in leadership have the principal responsibility of equipping others to do what they are doing, and as others grow, they can assume the mantle of leadership in the church. Practicing Christian education means that as we observe individuals maturing in their faith, we are also equipping them to serve as part of their faith formation.

Too Busy to Train Others?

Perhaps you're still laboring under the delusion that it's just easier if you do everything yourself. Training is not a high priority even when it is done. Jeffery Kiker and David Meir describe the rationale that Toyota Corporation has for training and equipping its workforce, making it one of the most successful companies in the world.[1] They identify the heinous error of thinking *we have no time to train*, which leads to ineffective training at best. With a lack of training, the workers are ineffective, and the quality of their work varies and is undependable. This means the administration of the corporation is almost always in a cycle of "firefighting." If left uncorrected, this creates a continual spiral downward in terms of productivity and quality of the product.[2] Ironically, the continuous firefighting is far more time consuming than the original training would have been. In short, valuing training and making sufficient time for it leads to effective training and hence workers who are effective and consistent in their results, and hence administration can depend on their work rather than having to solve problems.

The same is true for the church. Failure to train and equip volunteers, for whatever reason we may give, leads to ineffective volunteers who have little effect on the lives of those they are supposed to be serving. This in turn causes the pastoral staff and perhaps other leaders to continually step into conflict situations, fighting administrative fires and correcting problems that should have never occurred in the first place. Likewise, just as with Moses and the apostles, if we don't share the ministry by recruiting and equipping qualified individuals to serve, the potential of our ministry is limited to what can be accomplished by one individual, which sets us on a path for burnout. Practicing Christian education requires us to value those with whom we can share ministry, demonstrating our commitment to them and their call to serve as a volunteer by recruiting and equipping them to effectively serve.

Biblical Recruitment Principles

In Acts 6:1–7 the apostles are compelled by necessity to recruit and appoint a new set of volunteer leaders within the church in Jerusalem. This is the first time in the life of the church that the Twelve have to share the work of Christ with others. How do they do it? What principles can we discern for practicing Christian education today?

First, we need to recognize that the need for ministry is growing (6:1). If we deceive ourselves, thinking that we can do it all or that the ministry can somehow include just our own service, we'll never even attempt to recruit others. Christian educators need to be familiar enough with the congregation to recognize where ministry is not being done or is not being done effectively. Without this, the ministry will never be shared with others. What are potential ministry areas that are currently overlooked or understaffed?

Second, we need to practice the stewardship of our own mission (6:2). While needs may be evident, we must recognize what God has called us to do and be willing to bring along coworkers in Christ to serve alongside us. To do this, we have to have our own sense of mission and steward it, rather than letting it be buried in daily routines, workload, or responsibilities that could readily (or even more effectively) be filled by others. We are in essence locating like-minded individuals who hear a call to serve as a volunteer in a ministry for which we are responsible; we are preserving our call to serve while asking them to serve as well.

Third, we need to set qualifications for those who will serve (6:3). The church cannot have an anyone-will-do approach to service. When Christian educators resort to gimmicks like posters, newsletter notes, or appeals from the pulpit, quality control is abandoned. We need to set qualifications and earnestly pray for and seek individuals who fit them. What kind of qualifications? Some may focus on their beliefs; others may focus on their life and character. Another area of concern is relational abilities, since volunteers will undeniably be asked to work with others in the church. Giftedness is crucial; do they show the ability to perform what is conducive to the ministry? Make sure to write out these expectations. They should be kept to a core of about five items, but should be articulated so clearly that they can be written. We recruit those who exhibit a sincere faith in Christ, the potential to learn, and the disposition to serve.

Fourth, "pick out from among you" (6:3). Remember, volunteers and congregational leaders come from within the congregation. Ministries cannot indefinitely rest on outside assistance. Also, leaders should not be selected by one person, but rather by a group of leaders. Pool your spiritual and pastoral resources to determine whom to recruit as a volunteer to serve in the church's ministry. Recruitment is a personal, not mechanical, matter. It is people interacting, relating, and eliciting others to serve. Effective recruitment is first and foremost about building relationships within the congregation, relationships that later can become an avenue to discerning giftedness and fit for ministry.

Fifth, know how many you need (6:3). No, don't limit it to seven all the time just because Acts 6 did; but it is obvious that the apostles knew from prior experience that seven people could do the ministry. They did not under- or over-recruit for the task ahead of them. If qualified volunteers really are limited, and you don't want to under- or overutilize them, then knowing the optimal number you need in the group, class, program, or ministry is crucial for success. People are more likely to volunteer or respond affirmatively to an invitation to serve if they know how large the task is going to be and how many people they'd be working with.

Sixth, we are sharing ministry, not vacationing from it (6:4). The apostles made sure to explain to the congregation that by having volunteers serve, they were not going to back off their work; rather, the volunteers would allow them to stay faithful to their primary task. This is not the proverbial "working myself out of a job"; rather, it's ensuring that what God has called and gifted us to do will be accomplished because others are sharing in the ministry with us.

Seventh, participants are screened (6:5). Notice how the list of those selected adds information about them. "Stephen, a man full of faith and of the Holy Spirit, . . . and Nicolas, a proselyte of Antioch." They knew these men. They had been vetted. The congregation had presented them to the apostles, and the apostles obviously got to know them more, ensuring they were the right kind of individuals to participate in the ministry of the church.

Eighth, ministry volunteers are given approval and affirmation of leadership (6:6). If we are serious about valuing ministry and the participants in it, then a show of affirmation and approval is necessary. How do we show approval and affirmation to those who volunteer to serve alongside us in the teaching ministry? This was a public show of support for these seven men chosen and approved to serve.

Ninth, practicing Christian education requires us to check for results (6:7). In Acts 6:1, "the disciples were increasing in number," but now, with the new ministry design, "the number of the disciples multiplied greatly" (6:7). Practicing Christian education doesn't assume that decisions were faultless, plans were perfect, or that our selections for participants were always correct. Obviously in Acts 6 the problem of the Hellenistic widows was addressed, the principal mission of the apostles was preserved, and the ministry of the church expanded—to the end of a greater impact for God's Kingdom.

Realize that all these principles also outline the rationale for recruiting capable individuals. The best candidates are those who are suited to fit a recognized need, motivated to serve by not only identifying that need but being selected as a potential leader, vetted and affirmed by the ministry's leadership, and finally given the privilege and responsibility of serving in the church's ministry. But how do Christian educators do all this while continually equipping them to serve?

Equipping the Saints to Serve

One mode of equipping is never enough. Certain forms of training, teaching, orienting, and motivating require different formats. Regardless of how we do Christian education, these four modes can thoroughly equip volunteers with the necessary know-how, disposition, and skills to fulfill their ministry. What modes do we use to accomplish this?

Group Study

How do we learn? In classrooms! The most frequent means of delivering instruction in the history of the world is the classroom or, more generally, studying together as a group. In fact, when we think of practicing Christian education we probably picture a classroom. Even Jesus taught his disciples all together as a group, asking questions and explaining himself to them (Matt. 16:13–20; Mark 4:10), and when writing to congregations he had founded, Paul often reminded them that they too had been instructed by him together (1 Cor. 11:2, 23; 15:3; 2 Thess. 2:15). Group study, with or without walls, seems to be the most frequent means of equipping and training.

Group study is used best for a variety of outcomes, and all of them are cognitive. Such settings can be used to provide information to the group, orient them to a new task or opportunity, or explain what is new or changing in the ministry. Group study may take the form of routine meetings, meetings called as needed, or even a retreat/advance for volunteers, providing a more extended period for study and dialogue. Church leaders could perhaps study the Pastoral Epistles together, or perhaps volunteers in the next-generation ministries could study a book, a set of articles, or a video about children and adolescents. Group study equips believers to serve.

Mentor

Have you ever had that person who guided, directed, encouraged, and in essence poured into your life something from their own life? No classroom, no groups, just one-on-one, or perhaps a triad of believers being spiritually tutored by another. We see this in the relationship of Paul and Barnabas (Acts 4:36; 9:27; 11:26, 30, 12:25; 13:2, 7); we see it even more in Paul's relationship with Timothy, whom he calls "my true child in the faith" (1 Tim. 1:2; cf. 1 Cor. 4:17; 1 Tim. 1:18; 2 Tim. 2:1), and with Onesimus, whom Paul also regards as his son (Philem. 10). Paul's admonition to the believers at Corinth, "Be imitators of me, as I am of Christ" (1 Cor. 11:1), is an affirmation of mentoring as a means of equipping volunteers and leaders to serve in the church.

Mentoring gives rise to a sense of personal accountability and is almost always favored as a means of shaping individuals' values and character, leading to more affective outcomes than the group study can provide. It is not training for a skill or learning a new method but rather being equipped through a discipling relationship that provides spiritual direction as a means of maturing the volunteer.

Supervision

How do you best learn a new skill? In the classroom? Having an encouraging mentor? Or is it having a more capable teacher to instruct and guide you in how something is done step-by-step? This is supervision, like on-the-job training. Remember learning how to ride a bike? Odds are you didn't teach yourself, nor did someone lecture you about the history and philosophy of biking; rather, you were shown what to do, then you tried it for yourself with someone standing by to assist, and this continued until you were able to ride the bike without direct assistance. Supervision is the most effective means of equipping volunteers with the required skills to engage in their ministry.

Mark's depiction of Jesus's relationship to the disciples adequately illustrates supervision as a means of equipping others to serve. Early in Mark's Gospel, Jesus exclusively does ministry while the disciples are spectators, observing his work (Mark 1:14–3:12). Later, Jesus's disciples assist him in his work, taking a more active part in ministry (Mark 3:13–6:6). Then the disciples are capable of doing ministry under the direct supervision of Jesus (Mark 6:7–13, 30). Finally, they are commissioned to carry out the ministry themselves, without Jesus's physical presence (Mark 16:15–16, 20). Jesus trained the Twelve by providing a process of supervision.[3]

Supervision provides a context for spiritual formation through service to occur. Unlike with mentoring, the focus is more active—the acquiring of new skills needed in the ministry. It is showing someone step-by-step, with you at their side, how to do something they have never before done.

Self-Directed

Knowing how to teach requires a level of personal maturity and depth that we'd hope all our volunteer leaders could attain. The diligence and benefits of personal study are often mentioned in Scripture, especially regarding the Bible itself (Ezra 7:10; 2 Tim. 2:15). Christian educators can recommend or even supply materials for volunteers to read on their own. This actually might be the best use of a church library that anyone has considered! Just as personal study is essential for the pastoral staff in a ministry team, the volunteers serving with us benefit when they are equipped to study on their own. It keeps us all current with changes in methods of ministry, new scholarship on current issues, and developments in society and culture that shape the context of our service.

General Principle: 1–1–1–1. How can we pace ourselves adequately? To what can our self-directed preparations for ministry aspire? Is there a standard to employ? Perhaps the following four items will assist.

- *Read* one book per month. This doesn't have to be heavy theology or the latest biblical commentary; it could be a short book on leadership, small group ministry, discipleship, church membership, or even a Christian classic for personal edification. The Christian educator can provide a list or even the resources themselves for the volunteer's use.

- *Attend* at least one conference per year. National church conferences, regional or state conferences, or even a learning event sponsored by an area Christian college or seminary can likewise benefit volunteers both personally and in their service to the congregation. The ministry could sponsor a trip to such conferences or provide information and even scholarships for volunteers to participate. They would become exposed to new ideas and ways of doing ministry.

- *Subscribe* to one Christian magazine or journal. These resources are targeted toward a particular ministry venue and hence provide specific equipping for those in a given ministry. Once again, subscriptions could be made by the church and the resource shared to minimize costs.

- *Visit* one healthy church per year. Many individuals know only the church they are currently attending, with no exposure to congregations different or larger than theirs. Our ministry partners can be asked to visit congregations and experience those congregations' ministries as a recipient of service, preparing visitors to come back and share what they learned.

Personalized self-study keeps the mind open to new ideas, refusing to let it become set like concrete, and challenges personal assumptions. Self-study can aid in general learning, reinforcing all that has been done by the other three modes of equipping to serve.

When all four of these modes are utilized, you get a very well-rounded volunteer for your ministry. They are knowledgeable, self-aware/mature, skilled, and capable, as well as self-motivated to serve in the congregation. Resources to accompany all four modes could be managed by the church library, or even by the church website, which could provide a link to specialized resources for each ministry team. Practicing Christian education asks us to value those who partner in ministry with us and to provide for their continual spiritual formation as well as growth as a member of the ministry team.

Reflection Questions

1. Reflect on an occasion in which you were being recruited to serve. What made it appealing? What made it not so appealing? What can you learn from that?
2. How might recruitment according to biblical principles be done in your own ministry setting?
3. Which of the four ways of equipping people to serve have you utilized (group study, mentor, supervision, self-directed)? How did it/they benefit you?
4. In your own ministry, how might you use these four methods of equipping to fully develop those serving alongside you? Which might be the most difficult? Why?

Suggestions for Further Reading

Anderson, Leith, and Jill Fox. *The Volunteer Church: Mobilizing Your Congregation for Growth and Effectiveness*. Grand Rapids: Zondervan, 2015.

Ike, Deborah. *The Volunteer Management Toolkit (Church Edition)*. N.p.: Velocity Ministry Management, 2013.

Morgan, Tony, and Tim Stevens. *Simply Strategic Volunteers: Empowering People for Ministry*. Loveland, CO: Group Publishing, 2005.

Searcy, Nelson, and Jennifer Dykes Henson. *Connect: How to Double Your Number of Volunteers*. Grand Rapids: Baker Books, 2012.

Notes

Chapter 1: The Value of Christian Education

1. C. S. Lewis, *Mere Christianity* (San Francisco: Harper & Row, 2001), 40–41.
2. John G. Stackhouse, *Evangelical Landscapes* (Grand Rapids: Baker Academic, 2002), 71.
3. Ibid., 193.
4. George Gallup Jr. and Jim Castelli, "Americans and the Bible," *Bible Review* (June 1990). http://members.bib-arch.org/publication.asp?PubID=BSBR&Volume=6&Issue=3&ArticleID=18.
5. Stephen Prothero, *Religious Literacy* (New York: HarperCollins, 2007), 11.
6. David Van Biema, "The Case for Teaching the Bible," *Time*, April 2, 2007, 43.
7. Cf. www.barnagroup.com.

Chapter 2: Biblical Principles for Practicing Christian Education

1. John G. Stackhouse, *Evangelical Landscapes* (Grand Rapids: Baker Academic, 2002), 193.
2. Nili Shupak, "Learning Methods in Ancient Israel," *Vetus Testamentum* 53, no. 3 (2003): 424, 426.
3. Roy B. Zuck, "Education in the Monarchy and the Prophets," in *Evangelical Dictionary of Christian Education*, ed. Michael J. Anthony (Grand Rapids: Baker Academic, 2001), 232.
4. Shupak, "Learning Methods," 424.

Chapter 3: Theology for Practicing Christian Education

1. A. E. McGrath, ed., *Theology: The Basic Readings* (West Sussex, UK: Wiley-Blackwell, 2012), 12.
2. Albert C. Outler, "The Wesleyan Quadrilateral in Wesley," *Wesleyan Theological Journal* 20, no. 1 (Spring 1985): 7–18.
3. See Randy Maddox, *Responsible Grace: John Wesley's Practical Theology* (Nashville: Abingdon, 1994), 36–46.
4. Diane Leclerc and Mark A. Maddix, eds., *Essential Church: A Wesleyan Ecclesiology*, 2nd ed. (Kansas City, MO: Beacon Hill, 2014), 17–19.
5. Michael Lodahl, *The Story of God: A Narrative Theology* (Kansas City, MO: Beacon Hill, 2008), 218.
6. See Sara P. Little's five hypothetical roles that theology can have in Christian education. Sara Little, "Theology and Education," in *Harper's Encyclopedia of Religious Education*, ed. I. V. Cully and K. B. Cully (San Francisco: Harper & Row, 1990), 649–51.

Chapter 4: The History of Practicing Christian Education

1. Jack L. Seymour, *From Sunday School to Church School: Continuities in Protestant Church Education in the United States, 1860–1929* (New York: University of America Press, 1982).
2. James Riley Estep Jr., "Philosophers, Scribes, Rhetors . . . and Paul? The Educational Background of the New Testament," *Christian Education Journal*, 3rd series, vol. 2, no. 1 (Spring 2005): 30–47.

Chapter 5: Education as Christian

1. D. Campbell Wyckoff, "Theology and Education in the Twentieth Century," *Christian Education Journal* 15, no. 3 (1995): 12.
2. Jack L. Seymour, "The Clue to Christian Religious Education: Uniting Theology and Education," *Religious Education* 99, no. 3 (2010): 279, 284.
3. Cf. James Riley Estep Jr., "What Makes Education Christian?," in *A Theology for Christian Education*, ed. James Riley Estep Jr., Gregg R. Allison, and Michael J. Anthony (Nashville: B&H, 2008), 35–43; Estep, "Developmental Theories: Foe, Friend, or Folly?," in *Christian Formation*, ed. James Riley Estep Jr. and Jonathan Kim (Nashville: B&H, 2010), 37–62.
4. Romney Moseley, "Education and Human Development in the Likeness of Christ," in *Theological Approaches to Christian Education*, ed. Jack L. Seymour and Donald E. Miller (Nashville: Abingdon, 1990), 147.
5. These passages are regarded as supporting scriptural sufficiency as presented in John MacArthur, "Embracing the Authority and Sufficiency of Scripture," in *Think Biblically! Recovering a Christian Worldview*, ed. John MacArthur (Wheaton: Crossway, 2003), 21–35.
6. Ted Ward, "Facing Educational Issues (1977)," in *Reader in Christian Education Foundations and Basic Perspectives*, ed. Eugene Gibbs (Grand Rapids: Baker, 1992), 333. Please note: The authors of this textbook, Mark and Jim, both studied under Ted Ward at Trinity Evangelical Divinity School (Deerfield, IL).
7. Estep, "Developmental Theories," 46.
8. Adapted from Estep, "What Makes Education Christian?," 32–37.
9. Jean Piaget and Bärbel Inhelder, *The Psychology of the Child* (New York: Basic Books, 1966).
10. Ken Badley, "The Faith/Learning Integration Movement in Christian Higher Education: Slogan or Substance?," *Journal of Research on Christian Education* 3, no. 1 (1994): 13–33. Cf. also more recently Patrick Allen and Kenneth Badley, *Faith and Learning: A Guide for Faculty* (Abilene, TX: Abilene Christian University Press, 2014).
11. Badley, "Faith/Learning Integration Movement," 28.

Chapter 6: Christian Education as Ministry

1. This is the Greek term also used in the sense of "ministry" in the Septuagint (LXX), the Greek translation of the Hebrew Old Testament completed in Alexandria, Egypt, in the third century BC. See Exod. 31:10; 39:13; Num. 4:12, 26; 7:5; 2 Chron. 24:14 in the LXX.
2. Based on Kevin E. Lawson, "Former Directors of Christian Education—Why They Left," *Christian Education Journal* 14, no. 2 (Winter 1994): 58–60.

Chapter 7: Learning to Be a Christian

1. Gerhard H. Bussmann, "A Three-Fold Model of Religious Education Based on the Nature of Revelation," *Religious Education* 72, no. 4 (1977): 407.
2. Benjamin S. Bloom, ed., *Taxonomy of Educational Objectives, Handbook 1: Cognitive Domain* (New York: David McKay, 1956).

3. Karen L. Estep, "Following Topographical Details: Learning Theory and Curriculum," in *Mapping the Curriculum in Your Church*, ed. James Riley Estep Jr. (Nashville: B&H, 2011), 99–102.

4. Lawrence Richards, *A Theology for Children's Ministry* (Grand Rapids: Zondervan, 1983), 24–28.

5. Bussmann, "Three-Fold Model," 403–4.

6. Bussmann, "Three-Fold Model," 405.

7. David Krathwohl, Benjamin S. Bloom, and Bertram B. Masic, *Taxonomy of Educational Objectives, Handbook 2: Affective Domain* (White Plains, NY: Longman, 1964).

8. Cf. James Riley Estep Jr., "Childhood Transformation: Toward an Educational Theology of Childhood Conversion and Spiritual Formation," *Stone-Campbell Journal* 5, no. 2 (Fall 2002): 183–206.

9. William Yount, *Created to Learn*, 2nd ed. (Nashville: B&H, 2012), 243.

10. Lev Vygotsky, *Thought and Language*, ed. Alex Kozulin (Cambridge, MA: MIT Press, 1986); Vygotsky, *Mind in Society* (Cambridge, MA: Harvard University Press, 1978).

11. K. Estep, "Following Topographical Details," 99–102.

Chapter 8: Scripture as Formation

1. Mark Maddix and Richard Thompson, "Scripture as Formation: The Role of Scripture in Christian Formation," *Christian Education Journal* 9 (Spring 2012): S79–S93.

2. Sandra Schneiders, "Biblical Spirituality," *Interpretation* 56, no. 2 (2002): 136.

3. Douglas Burton-Christie, *The Word in the Desert: Scripture and the Quest for Holiness in Early Christian Monasticism* (New York: Oxford University Press, 1993).

4. Doug Hardy, "Lectio Divina: A Practice for Reconnecting to God's Word," *Preacher's Magazine: A Preaching Resource in the Wesleyan Tradition*, Lent/Easter 2009, 38–41.

5. John Wesley, preface to *Hymns and Sacred Poems, 1739*, in *The Works of John Wesley*, ed. Thomas Jackson (London: Wesley Conference Office, 1872; repr., Grand Rapids: Zondervan, 1958), 14:321.

6. Roberta Hestenes, *Using the Bible in Groups* (Philadelphia: Westminster, 1983), 15.

7. Ibid., 17.

8. Robert A. Traina, *Methodical Bible Study* (Grand Rapids: Zondervan, 1980), 7.

9. David L. Thompson, *Bible Study That Works* (Nappanee, IN: Evangel, 1994), 12.

10. James F. White, *Introduction to Christian Worship*, 3rd ed. (Nashville: Abingdon, 2000), 167.

11. Susan J. White, *Foundations of Christian Worship* (Louisville: Westminster John Knox, 2006), 15.

Chapter 9: Congregational Education and Formation

1. Charles Foster, *Educating Congregations* (Nashville: Abingdon, 1994), 13.

2. Ibid., 23–24.

3. Richard P. Thompson, *Acts: A Commentary in the Wesleyan Tradition*, New Beacon Bible Commentary (Kansas City, MO: Beacon Hill, 2015), 94–99.

4. John Wesley, preface to *Hymns and Sacred Poems, 1739*, in *The Works of John Wesley*, ed. Thomas Jackson (London: Wesleyan Conference Office, 1872; repr., Grand Rapids: Zondervan, 1958), 14:321.

5. Karen Powell and Chap Clark, *Sticky Faith: Everyday Ideas to Build Lasting Faith in Your Kids* (Grand Rapids: Zondervan, 2011).

6. A one-eared Mickey Mouse ministry is one part of the church that is functioning separate from the rest of the church. Graphically, the church would be represented as one large circle, with this separate ministry as a smaller circle abutting that larger circle (hence, the imagery of a one-eared Mickey Mouse).

7. Mark A. Maddix and Dean Blevins, eds., *Neuroscience and Christian Formation: The Integration of Science and Faith* (Charlotte: Information Age Publishing, 2016), 182–83.

8. John H. Westerhoff III, "A Discipline in Crisis," *Religious Education* 74, no. 1 (January–February 1979): 13.

9. John Westerhoff III, "Formation, Education, Instruction," *Religious Education* 82, no. 4 (1987): 578–91, here 582.

10. Ibid., 581.

11. Debra Dean Murphy, *Teaching That Transforms: Worship as the Heart of Christian Education* (Grand Rapids: Brazos, 2004), 10.

12. Ibid., 105.

13. Charles Foster, *Educating Congregations: The Future of Christian Education* (Nashville: Abingdon, 1994), 70–76.

14. Ibid., 45.

15. Ibid., 46.

16. Lester Ruth, "Word and Table: A Wesleyan Model for Balanced Worship," in *The Wesleyan Tradition: A Paradigm for Renewal*, ed. Paul W. Chilcote (Nashville: Abingdon, 2002), 138.

17. James Riley Estep Jr., "Childhood Transformation: Toward an Educational Theology of Childhood Conversion and Spiritual Formation," *Stone-Campbell Journal* 5, no. 2 (Fall 2002): 183–206.

18. Ibid.

Chapter 10: Christian Formation

1. Lewis Sperry Chafer, *He That Is Spiritual* (Grand Rapids: Zondervan, 1983).

2. Ibid.

3. Ken Botton, Church King, and Junias Venugopal, "Educating for Spirituality," *Christian Education Journal*, n.s., 1 (Spring 1997): 33–48.

4. Ibid., 36.

5. Ibid., 34–35.

6. Stephen Fortosis, "Theological Foundations for a Stage Model of Spiritual Formation," *Religious Education* 96, no. 1 (2001): 49–63.

7. John H. Westerhoff III, *Will Our Children Have Faith?*, 3rd ed. (New York: Morehouse Publishing, 2012).

8. James W. Fowler, *Stages of Faith* (New York: HarperCollins, 1985); Fowler, *Becoming Adult, Becoming Christian* (San Francisco: Jossey-Bass, 1999).

9. Greg L. Hawkins and Cally Parkinson, *Move: What 1,000 Churches Reveal about Spiritual Growth* (Grand Rapids: Zondervan, 2011).

10. F. LeRon Shultz and Steven J. Sandage, *Transforming Spirituality* (Grand Rapids: Baker Academic, 2006), 176–80.

11. Adapted from Jannette Bakke, *Holy Invitations* (Grand Rapids: Baker, 2000), 29.

12. Susanne Johnson, *Christian Spiritual Formation in the Church and Classroom* (Nashville: Abingdon, 1989), 123.

Chapter 11: Developmental Theory

1. See Perry Downs, *Teaching for Spiritual Growth: An Introduction to Christian Education* (Grand Rapids: Zondervan, 1984), 69–80.

2. See Dean Blevins and Mark A. Maddix, *Discovering Discipleship: Dynamics of Christian Education* (Kansas City, MO: Beacon Hill, 2010), 122–26.

3. Carol Gilligan, *In a Different Voice: Psychological Theory and Women's Development* (Cambridge, MA: Harvard University Press, 1982).

4. Ted Ward, foreword to *Nurture That Is Christian: Developmental Perspectives on Christian Education*, ed. James C. Wilhoit and John M. Dettoni (Grand Rapids: Baker, 1995), 7–17.

5. Mark A. Maddix, "Unite the Pair So Long Disjoined: Justice and Empathy in Moral Development," *Christian Education Journal* 8, no. 1 (2011): 46–63.

6. Blevins and Maddix, *Discovering Discipleship*, 142.

7. James E. Loder, *The Transforming Moment* (San Francisco: Harper & Row, 1981).

Chapter 12: Life Span Development

1. Erik H. Erikson, *The Life Cycle Completed: A Review* (New York: Norton, 1982).

2. Daniel J. Levinson et al., *The Seasons of a Man's Life* (New York: Ballantine Books, 1978); Levinson, *The Seasons of a Woman's Life* (New York: Ballantine Books, 1996).

3. Levinson, *Seasons of a Man's Life*, 55–59.

4. Jeffry Jensen Arnett, *Emerging Adulthood: The Winding Road from the Late Teens through the Twenties* (New York: Oxford University Press, 2004), 312.

5. Perry Downs, *Teaching for Spiritual Growth: An Introduction to Christian Education* (Grand Rapids: Zondervan, 1984), 157.

6. See Mark A. Maddix and Dean Blevins, eds., *Neuroscience and Christian Formation: The Integration of Science and Faith* (Charlotte: Information Age Publishing, 2016).

Chapter 13: Christian Education and Church Health

1. Carl F. George, *How to Break Growth Barriers: Capturing Overlooked Opportunities for Church Growth* (Grand Rapids: Baker, 1993).

2. James Riley Estep Jr., "The Healthy Elder," e2:effective elders ministries, 2014–2016 Presentation Series, www.e2elders.org.

3. Greg L. Hawkins and Cally Parkinson, *Move: What 1,000 Churches Reveal about Spiritual Growth* (Grand Rapids: Zondervan, 2011).

Chapter 14: Teaching for Discipleship

1. Parker Palmer, *The Courage to Teach: Exploring the Inner Aspects of the Teacher's Life* (San Francisco: Jossey-Bass, 1998), 2.

2. See Malcolm Knowles, *The Modern Practice of Adult Education* (Englewood Cliffs, NJ: Prentice Hall, 1980). Knowles developed four primary aspects of adult learners: self-directed, prior experience, readiness to learn, and orientation to learning. The term *andragogical* and its approach was developed in 1968 in Malcolm S. Knowles, "Andragogy, Not Pedagogy," *Adult Leadership* 16, no. 10 (1968): 350–52, 380.

3. David Kolb, *Experiential Learning: Experience as the Source of Learning and Development* (Englewood Cliffs, NJ: Prentice Hall, 1984).

4. Ibid., 38.

5. Bernice McCarthy, *The 4Mat System* (Arlington Heights, IL: Excel, 1980).

6. Jerome Bruner, *The Process of Education* (New York: Random House / Vintage Books, 1963).

7. Donald Joy, *Meaningful Learning in the Church* (Winona Lake, IN: Life and Light, 1969).

Chapter 15: Leading and Administrating Christian Education

1. Anne T. Fraker and Larry C. Spears, eds., *Seeker and Servant: Reflections on Religious Leadership; The Private Writings of Robert K. Greenleaf* (San Francisco: Jossey-Bass, 1996), 40.

2. George Cladis, *Leading the Team-Based Church: How Pastor and Church Staffs Can Grow Together into a Powerful Fellowship of Leaders* (San Francisco: Jossey-Bass, 1999), 4.

3. Ibid., 4.

4. See Reggie McNeal, *Practicing Greatness: Seven Disciplines of Extraordinary Spiritual Leaders* (San Francisco: Jossey-Bass, 2006); James M. Kouzes and Barry Z. Posner, *The Five Practices of Exemplary Leadership*, enhanced ed. (San Francisco: Wiley, 2011).

5. Norman Shawchuck, *How to Manage Conflict in the Church*, vol. 1, *Understanding Conflict* (Leith, ND: Spiritual Growth Resources, 1983), 36.

6. For a summary of styles of conflict management, see Daniel Eckstein, "Styles of Conflict Management," *Family Journal* 5, no. 4 (1997): 240–44.

Chapter 16: A Path toward Spiritual Maturity: Curriculum

1. Cf. James Riley Estep Jr., Roger White, and Karen Estep, *Mapping Out Curriculum in Your Church* (Nashville: B&H, 2011), for a comprehensive treatment of curriculum in Christian education.

2. Arthur K. Ellis, *Exemplars of Curriculum Theory* (Larchmont, NY: Eyes on Education, 2004), 4–7.

3. James E. Plueddemann, "Do We Teach the Bible or Do We Teach Students?," *Christian Education Journal* 10, no. 1 (1994): 73–81.

4. Johannes Van der Walt, "The Third Curriculum—from a Christian Perspective," *Journal of Research on Christian Education* 9, no. 2 (2009): 163.

5. Cf. Joseph Baily, "Evangelical Curriculum Development," *Religious Education* 75, no. 5 (1980): 539–45.

6. D. Campbell Wyckoff, *Theory and Design of Christian Education Curriculum* (Philadelphia: Westminster, 1961), 17.

7. Cf. James G. Henderson and Richard D. Hawthorne, *Transformative Curriculum Leadership*, 2nd ed. (Upper Saddle River, NJ: Prentice Hall, 1995), 181.

8. Leroy Ford, *A Curriculum Design Manual for Theological Education* (Nashville: Broadman, 1991), 246–48.

Chapter 17: Equipping for Service

1. Jeffery K. Kiker and David P. Meir, *Toyota Talent: Developing Your People the Toyota Way* (New York: McGraw-Hill, 2007), 10.

2. Ibid., 11–12.

3. James Riley Estep Jr., "Transforming Groups into Teams," in *Management Essentials for Christian Ministries*, ed. Michael J. Anthony and James Riley Estep Jr. (Nashville: Broadman & Holman, 2005), 333–48.

Scripture Index

Subject Index